RICARDO HAMBRA
TABLA FOR ALL

CW00952885

RICARDO HAMBRA

Tabla For All
Tabla Para Todos

A COMPLETE LEARNING METHOD FOR INDIAN TABLA PERCUSSION SET

MÉTODO COMPLETO DE APRENDIZAJE PARA SET DE TABLA DE LA INDIA

In loving memory of my sister Adriana Hambra.

A la memoria de mi hermana Adriana Hambra.

English Translation: Ricardo Hambra, revised by Lara Colorado and Carol McEvoy
Music typesetting, illustration and layout: Jorge Enrique Vallejo
Cover art by schultz+schultz Mediengestaltung, Wien, Austria
Printed by Kohlhammer und Wallishauser GmbH, Hechingen, Germany
Production: Veronika Gruber

Order No. 13025
ISBN 978-3-89221-127-3

TABLE OF CONTENTS

TABLA DE CONTENIDO

CHAPTER III

CAPÍTULO III

ACKNOWLEDGMENTS

To the Beloved One.

To all the Masters of Tabla technique – *Gharanas* – as well as to those who followed them, from whom I take much inspiration and fortitude.

To my family and all the friends who helped me along the way, thank you all!

I would like to especially thank master Ustad Zakir Hussain, a true 'wizard spirit' of the Indian Tabla sound, and my most important reference of this instrument, with whom I had the privilege to study. It was a few years ago at the Omega Institute in Rhinebeck, New York, in a five-day workshop. His presence and wonderful wisdom inspired myself and the others present there, to become better human beings, musicians and Tabla players.

AGRADECIMIENTOS

Al Bienamado.

A todos los maestros fundadores de las técnicas de Tabla – *Gharanas* – asi como a sus sucesores, de quienes recibo inspiración y fortaleza.

A la familia y a todos los amigos que me han ayudado a lo largo del camino, gracias!

Quisiera agradecer especialmente al maestro Ustad Zakir Hussain, un verdadero 'espíritu mágico' del Tabla de la India, y en mi opinión el referente actual más importante de este instrumento, y con quien tuve el privilegio de estudiar. Fue hace unos años, durante un workshop de cinco días en el Omega Institute en Rhinebeck, New York. Su presencia e increíble sabiduría nos inspiraron a mi y al resto de los presentes, a volvernos mejores personas, músicos e intérpretes de Tabla.

Friends and musicians I would also like to thank for their collaboration and support:

Sri Sathya Narayana Raju (SSSB), for his unconditional love and friendship. He initiated me to Indian music and philosophy;

Nicolas Muller, Patricia Ruiz Takata, Alvaro Forque, Haydee Consorti, Lara Colorado, Carol McEvoy, for their help at the beginning stages of *Tabla for All*;

Veronika Gruber, for believing in *Tabla For All*; Jorge Enrique Vallejo, for his expert advice on the design of *Tabla for All*. For both of you, a heartfelt Thank you!

Mike Amundson, Paul Livingstone, John Bergamo, Sri Shyam Sunder, Sri Koola Seela Nadan, John Adorney, Daya Rawat, Stuart Hoffman, Fuzzbee Morse, Alex Burke, Sri Mata Prasad Misra, Sri Subhash Dhunoohchand, Daniel Diaz, Juanjo Guillem, Eduardo Laguillo, Martin Cohen, Alejandro De Raco, Sergio Bulgakov, Ariel Chab Tarab, Eduardo Blacher, Aditya Varnam, etc. for their musical support as well as a positive part of my career as a musician, Thank you all!

Amigos y músicos a quienes también quiero agradecer su colaboración y soporte:

Sri Sathya Narayana Raju (SSSB), por su amor y amistad incondicional. El fue quien me inicio en la música y filosofía de la India;

Nicolás Muller, Patricia Ruiz Takata, Álvaro Forque, Haydee Consorti, Lara Colorado, Carol McEvoy, por su ayuda en los primeros pasos de *Tabla para Todos*;

Veronika Gruber, por creer en *Tabla para Todos*; Jorge Enrique Vallejo, por su consejo experto para el diseño de *Tabla para Todos*. Para ambos Muchas Gracias!

Mike Amundson, Paul Livingstone, John Bergamo, Sri Shyam Sunder, Sri Koola Seela Nadan, John Adorney, Daya Rawat, Stuart Hoffman, Fuzzbee Morse, Alex Burke, Sri Mata Prasad Misra, Sri Subhash Dhunoohchand, Daniel Diaz, Juanjo Guillem, Eduardo Laguillo, Martín Cohen, Alejandro De Raco, Sergio Bulgakov, Ariel Chab Tarab, Eduardo Blacher, Aditya Varnam, etc. por su aporte musical y positivo a lo largo de mi carrera. Muchas Gracias a Todos!

INTRODUCTION

First of all, thank you for your interest in this method, called *Tabla for All*. It's a complete training process towards learning what is considered one of the most outstanding percussion instruments that has ever existed: the Indian *Tabla* percussion set.

This wonderful instrument is included in the category of the *Kettle Drums*, obviously due to the shapes of both drums, especially the low-pitched drum or *Bayan*, which closely resembles the form of ancient clay kettles.

Sri Amir Khusró, a civil servant acting as head chancellor for the King Allaudin Khilji, created the Tabla in India around the 15th Century. Khusró was also an outstanding musician, musicologist and poet. Contributing greatly to the development of music and art in India, he invented among other things, the Tabla and the *Sitar*. He created the Tabla by modifying another percussion instrument called the *Pakhawaj*, which was used along with the *Mridangam* to accompany Indian folk chants and dances.

INTRODUCCIÓN

Ante todo, muchas gracias por su interés en este método titulado *Tabla para Todos*. En el veremos un proceso completo de aprendizaje y entrenamiento, para lograr conocer a fondo lo que es considerado uno de los instrumentos de percusión más completos que existen: el *Tabla*.

Este magnífico instrumento está incluido dentro del grupo de los denominados *Tambores Vasija*, ya que sus cuerpos – especialmente el *Bayan* o tambor grave – poseen una forma idéntica a las vasijas de barro antiguas.

El Tabla fue creado en la India alrededor del siglo XV por **Sri Amir Khusró**, un funcionario que desempeñaba el cargo de canciller jefe del rey Allaudin Khilji. Khusró era un destacado músico, musicólogo y poeta. Como gran colaborador en el desarrollo del arte y la música de la India fue el inventor del Tabla y el *Sitar*. Para crear el Tabla, modificó otro instrumento de percusión: el *Pakhawaj*, un tambor que se utilizaba junto al *Mridanga* para acompañar cantos y danzas del folklore de la India.

Mridangam

Tabla

Pakhawaj

The body of the Pakhawaj is made out of wood; on both sides of its body there are drumheads, which are joined to each other by a leather cord. In the Tabla, each of the Pakhawaj sides has become one of the two Tabla drums; the higher-pitched *Dayan*, and the lower-pitched *Bayan*. In order to play the Tabla, it must be placed horizontally on the floor, or over the musician's legs.

Unfortunately, the Tabla did not meet with success in the royal families of those days. It was used only to accompany dancing and some other musical styles such as *Gazal Gayak* and *Khayal*, where it was used as the lead instrument. Later on, the Tabla came into popular use through the contributions of **Ustad Uddar Khan** a musician who extracted a new terminology from the rhythmic language of the Mridangam and the Pakhawaj, and applied it to the Tabla according to the ancient laws that governed the *Talas* or Rhythmic Cycles, in Indian music.

Nowadays, the Tabla is key to the Indian musical culture and one of the most popular instruments, especially in the *Industani* music system of Northern India, where it is used in Solo concert performances and also as an indispensable rhythmic complement for other instruments,

El Pakhawaj posee un único cuerpo de madera en cuyos extremos se encuentran dos parches unidos por un tiento de cuero. En el Tabla, estos parches se traducen en los tambores agudo y grave, que actualmente se distinguen como *Dayan* y *Bayan*. Se ejecuta apoyado en el suelo o sobre las piernas del músico en forma horizontal.

Desdichadamente el Tabla no tuvo éxito en las familias reales de aquellos días. Su uso se limitaba a acompañar danza y algunos géneros musicales como el *Gazal Gayak* y el *Khayal*, utilizándose como primer instrumento. Posteriormente fue popularizado por **Ustad Uddar Khan**. Este músico extrajo del lenguaje del Mridanga y Pakhawaj una nueva terminología para ser utilizada en el Tabla, de acuerdo con las antiguas reglas que regían los *Talas* – ciclos rítmicos – de la música de la India.

En la actualidad el Tabla es una pieza clave y uno de los más populares instrumentos utilizados por todo el arte musical Indio, especialmente en el sistema *Indostánico* – India del Norte – siendo complemento rítmico indispensable de otros instrumentos como el *Sitar, Sarod, Sarangi, Santoor, Armonio,* o *Flauta Bansuri*, así como del canto y la danza.

such as the *Sitar, Sarod, Sarangi, Santoor, Harmonium,* or *Bansuri flute*, as well as for chants and dancing.

As a solo instrument, the Tabla has a long ancestral tradition of different techniques and schools called *Gharanas*. These schools have developed and passed on their teachings orally from generation to generation, under the patronage of their founders or the eldest musician in the "family" (literal translation of *Gharana*).

Como instrumento solista posee una tradición ancestral con diferentes técnicas y escuelas llamadas *Gharanas*, que han ido desarrollando sus enseñanzas oralmente de generación en generación, apadrinados por su fundador o el más antiguo miembro de esta "familia" (traducción literal de *Gharana*).

Musicians playing Indian Tabla set and Sitar
Músicos tocando Tabla y Sitar

In India, sons traditionally inherit their father's profession. This is how the Gharanas have formed, incorporating disciples and followers. The Gharana is named after the place where its founder lives.

There are six main schools considered to have made the greatest contributions to the development of Tabla repertory and styles.

These are: *Delhi, Lucknow, Farukhabad, Benares, Arjada* and *Punjab Gharana*.

In this method, we will be looking at a combination of styles from different Gharanas, product of my apprenticeship with different Tabla masters during several trips to India, such as the late Master **Sri Shyam Srivastava** (Punjab Gharana) and **Sri Mata Prasad Misra** (Benares Gharana); and in the USA courses with the great master **Ustad Zakir Hussain**. Also complementing with the study of audio-visual methods for learning Tabla, such as *Learning Tabla with Alla Rakha* by the late Tabla legend **Ustad Alla Rakha** of the Delhi Gharana, and *42 Lessons for Tabla*, by **Ustad Keramatullah Khan** of the Farukhabad Gharana, and also *Tabla I – II* by **Sri Avtar Vir**.

Another important contribution to the creation of this method as well as to my own growth as a musician has been the chance to play alongside and share with other Indian, European and American musicians and Tabla players.

To be considered a member of any specific Gharana or school of Tabla requires a specialization within that

En India es costumbre que los hijos hereden la profesión de sus padres. Así se han ido creando estos Gharanas, incluyendo discípulos y adeptos. Los Gharanas son nombrados según el lugar donde reside su fundador.

En la historia del Tabla, seis principales tradiciones son hoy reconocidas como las que han contribuido al desarrollo de repertorios y estilos.

Estas son: *Delhi, Lucknow, Farukhabad, Benares, Arjada,* y *Punjab Gharana*.

Lo que se verá en este método corresponde a una combinación de estilos, producto del aprendizaje y estudio con diferentes maestros durante diversos viajes a la India, como **Sri Shyam Srivastava** (Punjab Gharana), **Sri Mata Prasad Misra** (Benares Gharana); en USA con el gran maestro **Ustad Zakir Hussain**; y complementando con métodos audiovisuales como *Learning Tabla with Alla Rakha* por **Ustad Alla Rakha** (Delhi Gharana); *42 Lessons for Tabla* por **Ustad Keramatullah Khan** (Farukhabad Gharana); *Tabla I – II* por **Sri Avtar Vir**.

También ha sido de gran ayuda el intercambio musical y el compartir con otros tablistas y musicos de la India, europeos y americanos, tanto en el plano de crecimiento musical como en lo que se refiere a la creación de este método.

Es importante aclarar que para ser considerado miembro de algún Gharana en particular se requiere de una especialización dentro de esa escuela, casi imposible de conseguir por músicos que no sean nativos de la India. Además, aunque con contadas excepciones, se debe tener

school, which is practically impossible for any non-native musician. With rare exceptions, you must have some Indian lineage in order to form part of a Gharana. It has never been my intention to seek formal acceptance but rather to humbly continue trying to absorb as much as I, a Westerner, am capable of learning.

algún tipo de linaje Indio para entrar a formar parte de estas escuelas. Mi intención nunca ha sido integrar ningún Gharana, sino humildemente intentar aprender lo que como hombre occidental pueda y continúe pudiendo abarcar.

The author playing Tabla
El autor tocando Tabla

With this method, I hope to share with people of the western world some of the knowledge and experience I've collected throughout the years, and to pay tribute to Indian music, my teachers and their generosity. I feel the time has come to pass on all the knowledge that I have been privileged to acquire.

My main interest is to bring the basic principles of this wonderful instrument, the Tabla, closer to you. I hope this course will be a useful learning tool, and that you can put it to good use.

It's important to point out that *Tabla for All* has been written in two languages: English and Spanish. I have decided to present this method in both languages because I believe that both English and Spanish-speaking readers will find it useful to read and understand a text (or at least give it a try) in both languages.

It is also my humble desire to contribute to awaken an interest in the different languages spoken in America and the world.

Have a good and rhythmic journey!

Es mi intención con este método, el acercar al público occidental algo del conocimiento y la experiencia que he conseguido a través de los años; así también como un humilde homenaje a la música de la India, a mis maestros y a su generosidad; y así como he aprendido, quiero ahora también intentar transmitirlo.

Es mi principal interés poner a su alcance los principios básicos de este maravilloso instrumento: el Tabla. Espero que le sea útil y pueda aprovecharlo.

Es importante destacar que *Tabla Para Todos* ha sido escrito en dos idiomas: Inglés y Español. He estimado conveniente el presentar este método en ambas lenguas, por creer que tanto el público Anglosajón como Hispanopar-lante encontrarán interesante la posibilidad de leer y entender un texto (o al menos intentarlo) en ambos idiomas.

Es también un humilde deseo de despertar interes por los diferentes idiomas que pueblan America y el mundo.

Que sigan los Buenos Ritmos!

Some other ethnic percussion instruments from India are: Tavil, Khanjira, Ghatam and Khol.
Otros instrumentos de percusión étnica de la India son, entre otros: Tavil, Khanjira, Ghatam y Khol.

THE TABLA

Rhythm in Indian music forms a solid and well-defined platform upon which instrumentalists and performers can create and compose. In addition, as a code common to all musicians, the rhythm allows them to create complex combinations and rhythmic phrases, which always concur in some point of the *Tala* or rhythmic cycle that is being played.

The Tabla has its own language of sounds and onomatopoeias that can be recited as well as played. In India all musical instruments are made according to the local customs and traditions. For this reason, specific measurements and sizes vary depending on the place of origin.

With the passage of time, the Tabla drums have gradually become smaller, although sometimes a larger-sized *Dayan* is still traditionally played, especially to accompany vocal performances.

Nowadays the average high-pitched drum, the Dayan, is 10 – 12″ high. It is cylindrical and trapezoidal in shape; with a wider bottom 6 1/2 – 8″ in diameter and about 4 1/2 – 6″ across at the top. It is built from a single piece of wood, hollowed out until about half way down, leaving a shell, approximately 1/2″ thick, which forms the body of the drum.

The average low-pitched *Bayan* is about 10 – 12″ high, and 8 – 10″ across the top. A variety of different materials are used for the body, with a nickel/brass alloy being the most common nowadays. In former times, instruments were made of clay or brass, but however good the sound they produced, clay is too fragile, and copper too expensive to be practical.

On both drums there is a main leather thong or string called *Chot* that holds together the body and the *Gajra* (drumhead). The Dayan and Bayan drumheads are both similar (see illustration below):

EL TABLA

El ritmo en la música de la India constituye una base sólida y definida sobre la que los instrumentistas e intérpretes pueden crear y componer. Además es un código común a todos los músicos, ya que a través de éste se logran crear complejas combinaciones y frases rítmicas que siempre terminan coincidiendo en alguna parte del *Tala* – ciclo rítmico – que se está interpretando.

El Tabla posee un lenguaje propio de sonidos y onomatopeyas que puede ser tanto recitado como ejecutado en el instrumento. En la India los instrumentos musicales se fabrican de acuerdo con las costumbres locales y tradiciones, por lo cual las dimensiones y medidas específicas varían de acuerdo al lugar donde se fabrica.

Se sabe que a través del tiempo se ha ido reduciendo el tamaño de los tambores, aunque también continúa el uso tradicional del *Dayan* – tambor agudo – de mayor tamaño en el acompañamiento de algunas interpretaciones, principalmente vocales.

En la actualidad el Dayan mide aproximadamente entre 25 y 30 cm de alto. Es de forma cilíndrica y trapezoidal con una base más ancha, entre 16 y 20 cm de diámetro y de 11 a 15 cm en la parte superior. Está construido en una sola pieza de madera, ahuecada hasta la mitad, y dejando un ancho de entre 1 y 1.5 cm de espesor que constituye el cuerpo del tambor.

A su vez el *Bayan* – tambor grave – mide entre 25 y 30 cm de alto con un diámetro de aproximadamente 20 a 25 cm en su parte superior. Una variedad de materiales es utilizada en la construcción de su cuerpo. Una aleación de bronce/niquel es la más frecuente. Antiguamente se utilizaba barro o bronce que producían muy buen sonido, pero el barro se quiebra con facilidad y el cobre es demasiado costoso.

En ambos tambores se utiliza el llamado *Chot*, una cuerda de cuero que mantiene unidos al *Gajra* (parche), el cuerpo y la base de los mismos. Los parches o pieles del Dayan y Bayan son similares (ver ilustración):

DAYAN & BAYAN DRUMHEADS OR GAJRA

DAYAN & BAYAN: PARCHES O GAJRA

Pagri
external ring
anillo externo

Kinar
external circle
círculo externo

Shyahi
central circle
círculo central

Sur
middle circle
círculo medio

- There is the main skin, attached to which is another skin forming an external circle, *Kinar*.
- The central black paste patch is called *Shyahi* – central circle. This eliminates undesirable overtones and makes it possible to tune the drums.

The *Shyahi* patch is made of iron shavings mixed with a paste of different sorts of flours. Each manufacturer has his own formula so the composition differs throughout India. In the *Punjab* region for example a rice paste is sometimes used in the mixture instead of flour. The addition of iron shavings produces a permanent patch. The mixtures without iron shavings are not permanent and must be replaced or restored constantly. This is especially true of the ancient South Indian *Mridangam* and North Indian *Pakhawaj*.

The Shyahi are about 21/2 to 31/2 inches in diameter. The material is applied to the drumhead surface in layers of concentric circles so that the edge is thinner than the center of the Shyahi.

On the Dayan, the Shyahi is placed in the center of the drumhead; but on the Bayan it is set approximately 11/4 – 11/2" off-center.

The drumheads are made out of goat skin in layers; the external circle or *Kinar* skin, is stitched next to the edge by means of a fine leather strand, which is then interwoven with a heavy supporting leather ring called *Pagri*, which forms a rigid frame around the circumference of the drumhead.

- En ambos hay una piel principal a la que se adosa otra piel encima y alrededor del borde denominada *Kinar*.
- El centro del parche es de color negro, llamado *Shyahi* y está realizado en una pasta especial que elimina los armónicos no deseados y posibilita su afinación.

La composición del material para el *Shyahi* consiste en limadura de hierro mezclado con una pasta de harinas de diferentes clases – cada fabricante posee su propia fórmula por lo que la composición del Shyahi difiere a lo largo de toda India. En el *Punjab* por ejemplo, una pasta de arroz se utiliza a veces como parte de la mezcla en lugar de harina. El agregado de limaduras de hierro produce una mezcla permanente. Las mezclas que no lo poseen deben ser cambiadas o restauradas constantemente. Esta clase de mezcla se sigue utilizando en el *Pakhawaj* y el *Mridangam*, y debe ser removida cada tanto y cambiada.

El Shyahi posee un diámetro de entre 6 y 9 cm. Se aplica en la superficie de la piel en forma de capas que van decreciendo en tamaño a medida que se acercan al centro, de manera que los bordes son más finos y el medio del Shyahi más grueso.

En el Dayan, el Shyahi se ubica justo en el centro del parche, pero en el Bayan se desplaza del centro unos 3 o 4 cm.

La piel de los parches es de cabra y posee varias capas. La del círculo externo del parche – *Kinar* – es fijada junto al borde por una especie de tiento de cuero, que luego se trenza a un grueso anillo del mismo material. De esta manera se forma el marco rígido alrededor de la circunferencia del tambor, llamado *Pagri*.

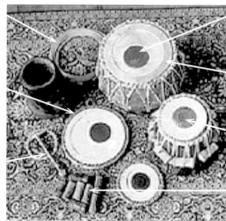

Chot
leather cord
cuerda de cuero

Pagri
leather ring
anillo de cuero

Hammer
tuning tool
martillo (para afinar)

Shiyahi
black circle
círculo negro

Kinar
external circle
círculo externo

Gajra
skin drumhead
parche

Gattha
cylindrical wooden pegs
tacos de madera cilíndricos

The entire drumhead or Gajra is attached to the body of the Dayan and Bayan drums, by a strong leather cord about 1/2" thick called *Chot*. The Chot is interwoven through the 16 holes placed around the Pagri at the top, then passes around underneath the drum through anoth-

El Gajra o parche es fijado al cuerpo de los tambores – Dayan y Bayan – por un tiento de cuero de aproximadamente 1 cm de ancho llamado *Chot*. Éste se entrelaza entre los 16 orificios que se encuentran alrededor del Pagri en la parte superior, y otro anillo de cuero ubicado

er leather ring called a *Gurri*. All parts work to hold the drumhead firmly against the body of the drum.

The Chot is tightened in such a way as to increase or decrease the pressure on the drumhead and thus change the tone. On the Dayan drum, cylindrical wooden blocks called *Gattha* are interlaced with the Chot. These are then struck with a hammer – upwards or downwards – to raise or lower the tension.

The Bayan drum has all the components of the Dayan drum, with the exception of these wooden blocks. However, similar wooden blocks can be added to the Bayan drum, when the Chot have stretched. Some Bayans incorporate a tensing system, consisting of a cotton cord, which can be tightened or released by means of metal rings.

en la base de los tambores llamado *Gurri*. Este trenzado hace que el parche se fije con firmeza al cuerpo del tambor.

La tensión del Chot varía de acuerdo con el tono con que se desee afinar el Tabla. En el Dayan, pequeños cilindros de madera llamados *Gattha* se colocan entrelazados al Chot, los cuales son luego golpeados con el martillo que se utiliza para afinar – hacia arriba o hacia abajo – para aflojar o incrementar la tensión del parche.

En el Bayan no hay Gattha de madera, aunque se le pueden agregar para subir el tono del parche si éste se encuentra poco tenso. Algunos Bayan poseen un sistema de tensión diferente que consiste en entrelazar, en lugar de un tiento de cuero, un cordón de algodón grueso junto a unas anillas de metal, de manera que al subir o bajar las anillas se aumenta o afloja la tensión del parche.

Bayan with cotton cord and metal rings.
Bayan con tensores de cuerda de algodón y anillos de metal

POSITIONING YOURSELF TO PLAY TABLA SET:

The Tabla player sits on the floor with their legs crossed and the Tabla in front. Both drums are placed on the floor over little circular cushions called *Adharas*, which make it possible to tilt the Bayan and the Dayan drums without sacrificing stability.

The Dayan is always tilted away from the player and sometimes a bit to the left, according to what is most comfortable for each player. The Bayan drum is usually placed with its drumhead parallel to the ground, but some musicians prefer to tilt it a bit, as they do with the Dayan.

Note: Remember that Rik is a left-handed Tabla player, therefore he positions the Dayan on his left side.

POSICIÓN PARA MÚSICOS Y ESTUDIANTES DE TABLA MAYORMENTE UTILIZADA:

El músico está sentado sobre el suelo con las piernas cruzadas y el Tabla delante. Los dos tambores van apoyados en el suelo sobre unos cojines llamados *Adharas*, que permiten inclinar el Bayan y el Dayan sin que su posición pierda estabilidad.

El Dayan siempre va inclinado hacia el lado opuesto del músico, de acuerdo a la postura que mejor se adapte a cada uno. El Bayan se coloca usualmente con el parche en posición paralela al suelo, aunque algunas personas prefieren inclinarlo un poco, de la misma manera que el Dayan.

Nota: Ricardo toca como zurdo, por lo tanto acomoda el Dayan a su izquierda.

This is the most common position for the Tabla player (Ricardo is a left-handed player)
Esta es la postura más común del Tablista (Ricardo toca como zurdo)

TABLA BOLS

LOS BOLS DEL TABLA

The syllables called *Bols* or strokes are used in Indian music to express the content of a musical phrase or composition. Bols serve as a substitute for staff notation, and are very useful for musicians and students to memorize entire compositions.

The Bol has been used as a kind of "oral tradition" for this particular kind of instruments by Indian percussionists for centuries, with the early *Pakhawaj*, *Mridangam*, *Dholak* and *Tabla* drums, to name a few, as well as by Indian dancers and players of other musical instruments of India.

Reciting these syllables – Bols – the musician expresses the technique and rhythmical development of the composition, and then transforms this recited composition into an instrumental performance.

Verbally, the Bols or strokes are spoken as different combinations of vowels and consonants that translate into a wide variety of musical sounds, depending on each instrument's particular quality. Bols also indicate right or left hand strokes individually, or simultaneous strokes by both hands. There is no literal translation for the bols and they only take on meaning within a musical context.

Although India is a subcontinent large enough to have an amazing variety of languages, dialects and cultural traditions, the Tabla Bols are generally understood and performed in a similar manner throughout the country. Each *Gharana* – music school or family – has its own techniques and styles, but the main Bols are essentially the same for all of them.

Estas sílabas llamadas *Bols* son utilizadas en música de la India para expresar el contenido de una frase o una composición musical. Estas reemplazan la forma de notación escrita en occidente con notas o pulsos, y son muy útiles para aprender de memoria un repertorio.

Los Bols vienen siendo utilizados como forma de "legado oral" desde hace siglos por percusionistas de los más conocidos instrumentos de percusión de la India: *Pakhawaj*, *Mridangam*, *Dholak* y *Tabla* entre otros; asi como también por bailarines e instrumentistas de la cultura musical India.

Con el recitado de estas sílabas – Bols – el músico expresa tanto la técnica como la rítmica que comprende una composición para posteriormente transformar lo recitado en una interpretación instrumental.

Los Bols se diferencian para el oyente combinando consonantes y vocales que brindan una variedad de sonidos de acuerdo a cada instrumento. También se distinguen unas y otras para las diferentes manos individualmente y para los golpes combinados de ambas a la vez. Pero solo poseen significado dentro del contexto musical, ya que no tienen traducción literal.

Los Bols del Tabla son interpretados de manera uniforme a lo largo de toda la India, salvo algunas diferencias particularmente entre las prácticas y estilos de los distintos *Gharanas* – familias o escuelas musicales –, pero esencialmente los golpes principales son los mismos. Difieren en la pronunciación y los patrones rítmicos y fraseos que cada Gharana utiliza, producto de la gran variedad de lenguas y dialectos que existen en la India.

The author playing Tabla while reciting Bols, during a
performance of one of his compositions for vocal percussion and Tabla set
*El autor en concierto, tocando Tabla y recitando Bols a la vez,
en una de sus composiciones para set de Tabla y percusión vocal*

The following section, is comprised of detailed explanations of some *Bols*, their names, and hand and finger positions for their correct performance on the Tabla, along with graphic examples, depicting the place on the leatherhead where the Bols should be played.

Esta sección contiene explicaciones detalladas de algunos *Bols* – golpes –, sus nombres y posturas de manos y dedos para tocarlos de forma correcta en el Tabla. Además, se muestran ejemplos gráficos, describiendo el lugar sobre el parche donde los Bols deben tocarse.

DAYAN BOLS *High-Pitched Drum*

Playing position for the Dayan: Place the fingertip of your right-hand ring finger (left for left handed) touching the middle circle or *Sur* of the drumhead (pictures *A*, *B*).

    The ring finger acts as axis for your hand, maintaining it in contact with the drumhead. It is also possible to keep your little finger on the middle circle alongside the ring finger, or placed on the *Pagri* – external ring – as in other techniques (see *C* and *D*).

BOLS DEL DAYAN *Tambor Agudo*

Posición para tocar el Dayan: Colocar la yema del dedo anular (ver fotos *A*, *B*) de la mano derecha – o izquierda, dependiendo de la habilidad natural del ejecutante – apoyando sobre el circulo medio – *Sur* – del parche.

    Notar que el dedo anular actúa como un eje para la mano, manteniéndola constantemente en contacto con el parche. También es posible apoyar el dedo meñique junto al anular en el circulo medio, o en el *Pagri* – anillo externo del parche (*C* y *D*).

A
B
C
D

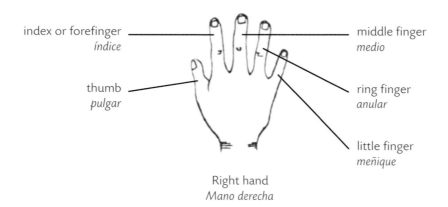

index or forefinger
índice

middle finger
medio

thumb
pulgar

ring finger
anular

little finger
meñique

Right hand
Mano derecha

Note: All the pictures for this method have been taken from a left-handed Tabla player. Please take notice of this fact, and apply the correct positioning for right-handed players.

Nota: Todas las imágenes para este método han sido tomadas de un Tablista zurdo (el Dayan se encuentra del lado izquierdo). Tenerlo en cuenta para las personas diestras (invertir la postura).

TA or **NA**: For this Bol or stroke, rest the fingertip of your ring finger on the middle circle – *Sur* – of the drumhead (see picture 1), while striking the external circle – *Kinar* – with your index finger (picture 2). The ring finger acts as a pivot, in contact with the drumhead. Your little finger can also remain on the Kinar, as reinforcement for the ring finger.

The **TA** Bol is the main stroke of the Dayan drum and is often used to tune the high-pitched instrument. The Bol produces a resonant, expanded sound.

EXAMPLE 1: TA OR NA

TA O NA: Para producir este Bol se apoya la yema del dedo anular sobre el círculo medio – *Sur* – del parche (imagen 1), mientras se golpea con el dedo índice el círculo externo – *Kinar* (imagen 2). El anular actúa como pivote manteniéndose en contacto con el parche; también puede utilizarse el dedo meñique sobre el Kinar acompañando al anular en su función.

Este golpe produce el sonido principal del Dayan, y también se utiliza mucho para afinar el tambor. El **TA** es un Bol resonante de sonido abierto.

EJEMPLO 1: TA O NA

TRACK
01
DISK
01

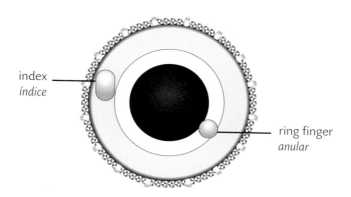

index
índice

ring finger
anular

1

2

TE: This Bol is performed by striking the middle circle of the drumhead – Sur – with the index finger, while keeping the ring finger in the same position as in the **TA** Bol. This Bol has a non-resonant, contracted sound.

Note: There is a variation of the **TE** *Bol, when it is used with another Bol such as* **TI** *in a sequence called* **TITE**, *which will be explained later in this method.*

TE: Este Bol se obtiene golpeando el círculo medio del parche – Sur – con el dedo índice y manteniendo el anular apoyado en el mismo sitio que con el **TA**. Es un Bol de sonido cerrado no resonante.

Nota: Otra variante del Bol **TE** *se da cuando se utiliza con otro Bol en secuencia, por ejemplo:* **TITE**, *que se explicará más adelante.*

EXAMPLE 2: TE

EJEMPLO 2: TE

TRACK
02
DISK
01

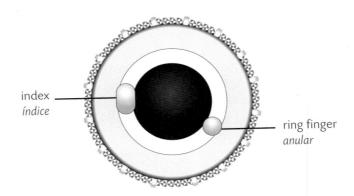

index
índice

ring finger
anular

1

2

TI: For this Bol strike the black central circle – *Shyahi* – with the middle finger, while keeping the ring finger in the same position as in **TA** and **TE**. It's also possible to play **TI** with the index finger, in which case this **TI** is used in combination with other Bols played in a sequence, for example: **TITE** that will be explained later.

This Bol produces a non-resonant, contracted sound.

TI: Este Bol se produce golpeando el círculo central – *Shyahi* – con el dedo medio y manteniendo el dedo anular apoyado sobre el Kinar como en **TA** y **TE**. También se puede golpear con el dedo índice, siendo este una variante cuando se combina con otro bol en secuencia, por ej. El **TITE**, que se explicará más adelante.

El Bol **TI** es un golpe no resonante de sonido cerrado

EXAMPLE 3: TI

EJEMPLO 3: TI

TRACK
03
DISK
01

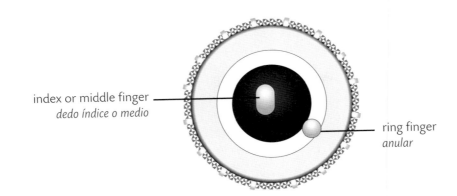

index or middle finger
dedo índice o medio

ring finger
anular

Note: The index finger is used most of all, in the early stages of Tabla training. Once you have spent sufficient time practicing all the Bols described for the Dayan drum with your index finger, then start using the middle finger for Bols like TI *or* TITE. *This progressive way of learning allows the student to get familiar with the Tabla technique step by step, gradually enhancing each finger's skill.*

TIN or TU (pronounces 'too'): For this Bol, strike the Shyahi or black central circle of the drumhead with your index finger, flicking your wrist and letting your finger bounce back after the stroke is made. In this Bol, your ring finger does not rest on the Kinar – middle circle – but remains in the air along with your other fingers, following the movement of your entire hand.

This Bol produces a resonant, expanded sound, and is also used like TA to tune the Dayan drum, because its sound allows the drum's whole range of harmonics to be heard.

Nota: El índice es el dedo más utilizado en la primera etapa del aprendizaje. Una vez estén bien practicados los golpes con este dedo, se incluye la práctica con el dedo medio en Bols como TI *o* TITE. *Esta forma gradual de aprendizaje se establece con la intención de ir ampliando de forma paulatina la habilidad de cada dedo en la ejecución de los Bols.*

TIN O TU: Este Bol se produce golpeando con el dedo índice sobre el círculo central – Shyahi –, haciendo un rápido movimiento con la muñeca y dejando que el dedo rebote sobre el parche sin permanecer en este luego del golpe. En este Bol el dedo anular no se apoya sino que queda en el aire acompañando el movimiento de toda la mano.

Es un Bol resonante de sonido abierto y también se utiliza (al igual que TA) para afinar el Dayan, ya que permite que se escuchen todos los armónicos que posee.

EXAMPLE 4: TIN OR TU

EJEMPLO 4: TIN O TU

TRACK
04
DISK
01

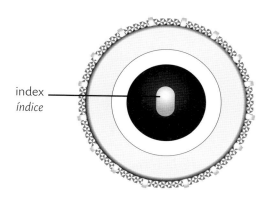

index
índice

MULTIPLE BOLS

TITE or **TETE**: This is a 2-stroke sequence very often used in rhythmic phrases within this method. It is produced by first striking the Bol **TI** on the Shyahi or black circle with your index finger. Then, follows the Bol **TE** with both middle and ring fingers together.

This **TITE** sequence can also be inverted at the musician's discretion by striking first with the middle and ring finger together and then with the index finger.

This Bol produces a non-resonant, contracted sound.

Note: Practice this sequence over and over to acquire confidence, speed and precision. It is better to start slowly with the TI and TE, TI – TE, etc, and then increase the speed bit by bit as you feel more comfortable with them.

BOLS MÚLTIPLES

TITE o **TETE**: Esta es una secuencia de 2 golpes muy utilizada en las frases rítmicas de este método. Se produce golpeando el círculo central – Shyahi – con el dedo índice, como se explicó anteriormente (**TI**), y luego los dedos medio y anular juntos (**TE**).

TITE también puede tocarse invirtiendo el orden de los golpes, a discreción del intérprete. En este caso se utilizarían primero los dedos medio y anular juntos, seguidos por el índice.

Estos golpes son no resonantes de sonido cerrado.

Nota: Practicar esta secuencia de golpes una y otra vez, hasta sentirse cómodo con el TI luego el TE, TI – TE, etc. Luego se puede ir incrementando la velocidad sin perder precisión.

EXAMPLE 5: TITE OR TETE

EJEMPLO 5: TITE O TETE

TRACK **05** DISK **01**

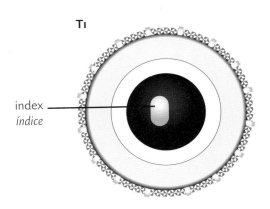

TI

index
índice

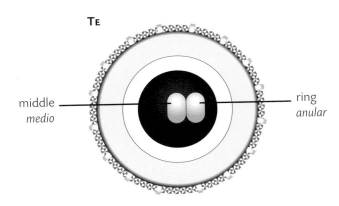

TE

middle
medio

ring
anular

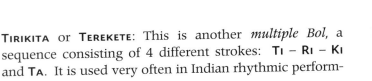

1　　2　　3

TIRIKITA or **TEREKETE**: This is another *multiple Bol*, a sequence consisting of 4 different strokes: **TI** – **RI** – **KI** and **TA**. It is used very often in Indian rhythmic performances.

First comes the **TI** Bol (the same bol as in **TITE**), by striking the Shyahi or black central circle with middle and ring fingers at the same time; then comes the **RI** Bol striking with your index finger on the same place, like the Bol **TE** in **TITE**. Then comes the **KI** Bol, which is played with the other hand (see *Bayan Bols*), and finally the **TA** Bol, which is played the same way as the first **TI** of the sequence.

All of these strokes should be played in quick sequence. Practice them over and over again, first slowly then faster,

TIRIKITA o **TEREKETE**: Otro *Bol compuesto*; una secuencia de 4 golpes: **TI** – **RI** – **KI** – **TA**. Su uso es muy común en interpretaciones rítmicas de la India.

El **TI** se golpea con los dedos medio y anular sobre el Shyahi (al igual que en **TITE**), luego el **RI** con el dedo índice también sobre el Shyahi o círculo central (de nuevo como **TITE**), luego el Bol **KI** con la otra mano (ver *Bols del Bayan*); por último el Bol **TA** – igual que el Bol **TI** del principio de esta secuencia.

Todos estos golpes se tocan en rápida sucesión. Se practica repitiendo la secuencia de lento a más rápido hasta obtener una sucesión de golpes uniforme y pareja:

until it feels like a uniform, even chain of sounds. First slow: **Tɪ – Rɪ – Kɪ – Tᴀ – Tɪ – Rɪ – Kɪ – Tᴀ**, etc. Then try faster: **TɪʀɪᴋɪᴛᴀTɪʀɪᴋɪᴛᴀTɪʀɪᴋɪᴛᴀTɪʀɪᴋɪᴛᴀ**, etc.

This Bol produces a non-resonant, contracted sound.

Tɪ – Rɪ – Kɪ – Tᴀ – Tɪ – Rɪ – Kɪ – Tᴀ, etc. Luego: **TɪʀɪᴋɪᴛᴀTɪʀɪᴋɪᴛᴀTɪʀɪᴋɪᴛᴀ**, etc.

Los golpes de este Bol son todos no resonantes de sonido cerrado.

EXAMPLE 6: TIRIKITA OR TEREKETE

EJEMPLO 6: TIRIKITA O TEREKETE

TRACK 06 DISK 01

Tɪ

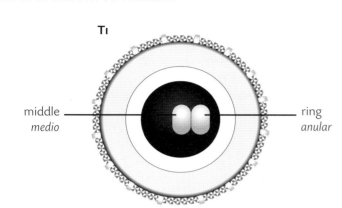

middle
medio

ring
anular

Rɪ

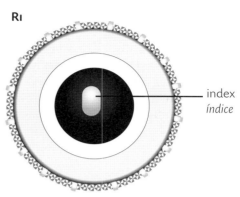

index
índice

Kɪ (or Kᴇ)

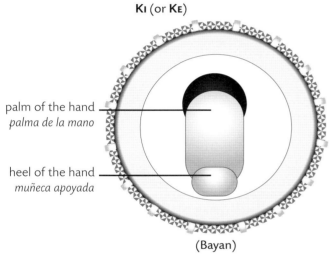

palm of the hand
palma de la mano

heel of the hand
muñeca apoyada

(Bayan)

Tᴀ

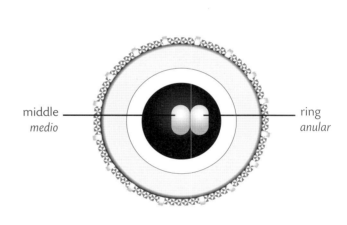

middle
medio

ring
anular

Tɪ – Dayan

1

Rɪ – Dayan

2

Kɪ (or Kᴇ) – Bayan

3

Tᴀ – Dayan

4

BAYAN BOLS *Low pitched drum*

The *Bayan Bols* contain 2 subgroups: *resonant Bols* and *non-resonant Bols*. Each of these groups has a special space in the rhythmic structure of Indian music. They are often related to the alternating Bols produced when you arrive at the "empty beat" or *Khali Vibhag*. It exists in every *Tal* – rhythmic cycle – within the Indian music system.

Understanding this part of the Tabla and Indian rhythmic system is very important, and we'll refer more extensively to the Khali Vibhag later in this method.

Now, let's go on to a practical description of the hand's finger names and the Bayan Bols, starting with the Bol **Ge**.

BOLS DEL BAYAN *Tambor grave*

En este grupo de Bols se distinguen los *Bols resonantes* y los *Bols no resonantes*, que corresponden en algunos casos a la alternancia de Bols que se produce al llegar al llamado *Khali Vibhag* o "compás vacío" de la acentuación rítmica que poseen todos los *Talas* – ciclos rítmicos – en la música de la India.

La comprensión de este tema es muy importante. Más adelante hay un comentario especial explicando con detalle el significado y lectura del Khali Vibhag.

Nos referiremos ahora a la descripción práctica de estos Bols, comenzando por los nombres de los dedos de la mano izquierda y siguiendo con el Bol **Ge**:

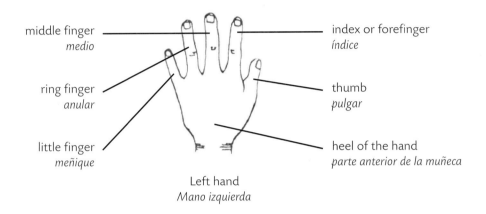

middle finger / *medio*

index or forefinger / *índice*

ring finger / *anular*

thumb / *pulgar*

little finger / *meñique*

heel of the hand / *parte anterior de la muñeca*

Left hand / *Mano izquierda*

Playing position for the Bayan: Place the heel of your hand on the center of the Bayan drumhead, then strike the *Sur* – the space between the *Shyahi* or black circle and the *Kinar* or external circle – with the fingertip of either your middle or index finger.

Note: Let your hand rest on the Bayan when not playing.

Ge or **Ga**: This Bol is the most important stroke of the Bayan drum, and sometimes is the "signature stroke" for the Tabla player, because of its distinctive sound. The Bol **Ge** is produced by striking the drumhead with the fingertip of your middle or index finger over the Sur or middle circle, between the Kinar and the Shyahi.

The Sur of the Bayan drumhead is often small, because the Shyahi is placed off-center, unlike the Dayan where all the circles or parts of the head are concentric. This allows the heel of the hand and wrist to push and release the center of the head, and produce the characteristic *glissando* sound of the **Ge** Bol.

Note that the middle finger is used more often than the index finger to perform this Bol. The index finger is used for fast performances, so it can interact with the middle finger. The finger movements are quick and energetic, allowing the finger to strike and bounce back off the drumhead. This technique requires patient, steady prac-

Posición para tocar el Bayan: Apoye la parte anterior de la muñeca en centro del parche y golpee el *Sur* – espacio entre el *Shyahi* y el *Kinar* o círculo medio – con la yema del dedo medio o del dedo índice.

Nota: Se sugiere dejar apoyada la mano sobre el Bayan cuando no se esté tocando.

Ge o **Ga**: Este es el bol más importante del Bayan, y en algunos casos se considera como el Bol característico del tablista, por su particular sonido. El Bol **Ge** se produce golpeando con la yema del dedo medio o el dedo índice, sobre la franja media o Sur, entre el Kinar y el Shyahi.

El Sur del Bayan es frecuentemente más pequeño, porque al Shyahi se encuentra desplazado unos centímetros del centro, a diferencia del Dayan donde todos los círculos o partes del parche son concéntricos. Esto permite a la zona del dorso de la mano y la muñeca presionar y soltar el centro del parche, y así producir el característico sonido *glissando* del Bol **Ge**.

Tener en cuenta que el dedo medio se utiliza más frecuentemente que el índice al tocar este Bol. El índice se utiliza para las partes rápidas, en las que interactua con el dedo medio. El movimiento de los dedos es rápido y enérgico, haciéndolos así golpear y rebotar del parche. Esta técnica requiere paciencia y práctica constante hasta

tice until the right sound is achieved. It produces a resonant, expanded sound.

lograr el sonido correcto. Se produce así un Bol resonante de sonido abierto, expandido.

EXAMPLE 7: GE OR GA

EJEMPLO 7: GE O GA

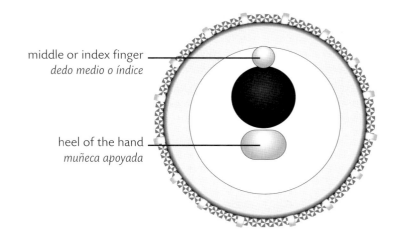

middle or index finger
dedo medio o índice

heel of the hand
muñeca apoyada

The **GE** *Bol from a different perspective*

El Bol **GE** *desde otra perspectiva*

Changing the Pitch of the Bol GE

This technique is one of the most highly esteemed in the art of Tabla playing. It is produced by lightly pressing the drumhead with the heel of your hand, right before or after the Bol has been played. In this way the pitch can be raised or lowered, as you have probably heard in some recordings and live performances.

This feature resembles the sound of the Bayan to the bass guitar because it has a range of about an octave from its original pitch. It's a form of *glissando*, and depending on each musician's expertise this feature can be incorporated to the repertoire of Talas (rhythmic cycles) and improvisations, in order to embellish and enhance the quality of the performance.

KE or **KI**: This Bol is produced by striking the drumhead with an open hand while keeping the back of the wrist in contact with the surface. It is relatively easy to play, and the sound is non resonant and contracted.

EXAMPLE 8: KE OR KI

Cambiando el tono del Bol GE

Esta técnica es una de las más valoradas características del arte de tocar Tabla. Se realiza empujando suavemente con la parte anterior de la muñeca, justo antes o luego de haber producido el Bol. De esta manera el golpe se puede hacer modular a más agudo o grave, como seguramente algunos de ustedes habrán tenido la oportunidad de oír en conciertos y grabaciones.

Esta característica hace que el sonido del Bayan se parezca a un 'Bajo', porque tiene un rango aproximado de una octava partiendo de su sonido original. Es una forma de *glissando*, y dependiendo de la habilidad de cada músico, esta técnica puede ser incorporada a los Talas (ciclos rítmicos) e improvisaciones, con la intención de embellecer y elevar la calidad de la interpretación.

KE o **KI**: Este Bol se produce golpeando con toda la mano abierta sobre el parche, y manteniendo la parte anterior de la muñeca en contacto sobre este. Es un Bol bastante sencillo de tocar, y su sonido es no resonante o de sonido cerrado.

EJEMPLO 8: KE O KI

TRACK 08 DISK 01

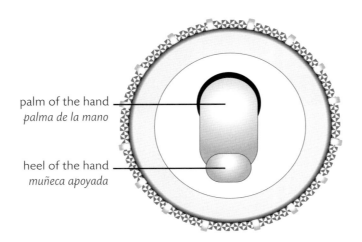

palm of the hand
palma de la mano

heel of the hand
muñeca apoyada

1

2

KA: This Bol is produced by half-closing your hand and dryly striking the Shyahi – black circle of the drum head – with the forepart of your four fingers (knuckles to nails) while resting the wrist on the drumhead. This Bol has a non-resonant and strong, dry sound.

It's also possible to combine the **KA** Bol with the Dayan Bols **TIN** or **TA**. If played together, a stronger accent is achieved.

KA: Este Bol se produce golpeando con la parte anterior de los 4 dedos, – nudillos y uñas – semicerrando la mano, sobre el circulo negro – Shyahi –, manteniendo la parte anterior de la muñeca apoyada sobre la superficie del parche. Es un Bol no resonante y de sonido fuerte y seco (sonido cerrado).

También es posible combinar el Bol **KA** con el Bol **TIN** o **TA** del Dayan. Al tocarlos simultáneamente se logra un sonido más acentuado y fuerte.

EXAMPLE 9: KA

EJEMPLO 9: KA

TRACK
09
DISK
01

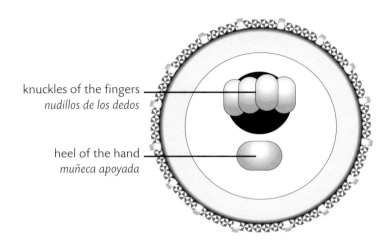

knuckles of the fingers
nudillos de los dedos

heel of the hand
muñeca apoyada

1

2

KAT: This Bol is played by striking with the whole open hand from up above the drum. In this case, unlike the **KE**, the back of the wrist doesn't rest upon the head, and the stroke comes straight from the air. Also, after the stroke is done, your hand does not bounce off, but remains in contact with the drumhead.

The sound of this Bol is non-resonant and dry or contracted.

KAT: Este Bol se produce golpeando con toda la mano abierta y por encima del tambor. A diferencia del **KE**, la parte anterior de la muñeca no está apoyada sobre la superficie, sino que el golpe proviene desde el aire, sin apoyo. Luego del golpe la mano no rebota sino que permanece en contacto sobre el parche.

El sonido de este Bol es no resonante y seco o contraido.

EXAMPLE 10: KAT

EJEMPLO 10: KAT

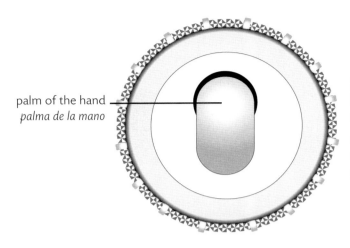

palm of the hand
palma de la mano

in this stroke the heel of the hand isn't initially in contact with the drumhead, unlike the **Ke** Bol

*en este golpe la muñeca de la mano no está apoyada en el parche, como en el Bol **Ke***

COMBINED BOLS

These Bols are the result of a simultaneous performance of Dayan and Bayan Bols with both hands. Since all of them include the Bol **GE**, the sound produced is resonant, open and expanded. Some of them are:

DHA: TA + GE, this is one of the most widely played combined Bols.

EXAMPLE 11: DHA

BOLS COMBINADOS

Estos Bols son el resultado de la interpretación simultánea de Bols del Dayan y el Bayan con ambas manos. Al estar incluído el **GE** en todos, son resonantes de sonido abierto y expandido. Algunos de estos son:

DHA: TA + GE, es generalmente uno de los Bols (o golpes) combinados más utilizado.

EJEMPLO 11: DHA

GE

TA

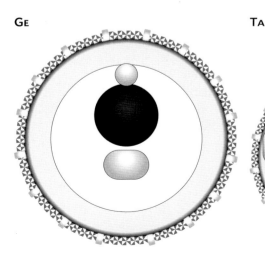

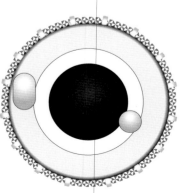

playing the Bol **Dha**
tocando el Bol **Dha**

DHE: Comes from the combination of Bols **TE** + **GE**.

EXAMPLE 12: DHE

DHE: Resulta de la combinación de los Bols **TE** + **GE**.

EJEMPLO 12: DHE

GE

TE

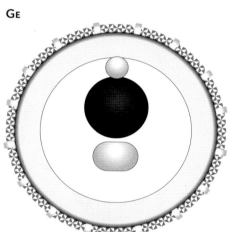
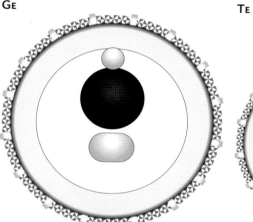
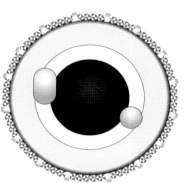

DHI: comes from the combination of Bols **TI** + **GE**

EXAMPLE 13: DHI

DHI: Resulta de la combinación de los Bols **TI** + **GE**.

EJEMPLO 13: DHI

GE

TI

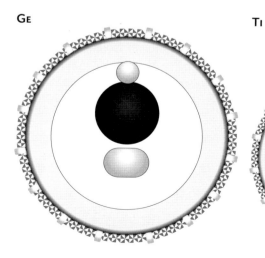
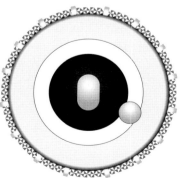

playing the Bol **Dhi**
tocando el Bol **Dhi**

Dhin: Comes from the combination of Bols **Tin** + **Ge**.

Dhin: Resulta de la combinación de los Bols **Tin** + **Ge**.

Example 14: Dhin

Ejemplo 14: Dhin

Track **14** **DISK** **01**

Ge

Tin

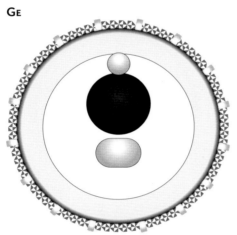

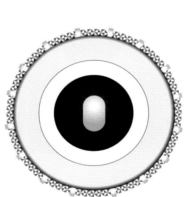

Note: Again, all these Combined Bols *are the result of two strokes played simultaneously. It's important to practice each Bol separately until you get a clear and correct sound. For example: Take the* **Ta** *first and practice it by itself; then take* **Ge** *and practice it by itself. Afterwards, practice them simultaneously, producing the Bol* **Dha**. *Keep working on it until you get the correct sound, like the one in the CD example. Repeat this process with the whole list of Combined Bols.*

Nota: Nuevamente, cada uno de estos Bols Combinados *es el producto de dos golpes tocados al mismo tiempo, simultáneamente. Es importante practicar cada uno de ellos por separado hasta lograr un sonido claro y correcto. Por ejemplo: Tomar primero el Bol* **Ta** *y practicarlo; Luego hacer lo mismo con el Bol* **Ge**. *Posteriormente practicar los 2 Bols y tocarlos simultáneamente, produciendo el Bol* **Dha**. *Continuar trabajando sobre éste hasta que suene de forma correcta, como en el ejemplo del CD. Repetir el proceso con la lista entera de Bols Combinados.*

EXERCISES FOR PRACTICE

The following exercises are intended to help develop the technique skills and the reading of the different combinations. Let's start with simple phrases, like the first one, and then practice the remaining exercises. These are not rhythmic cycles or Talas, but only examples for training and practice purposes. Talas will be shown later in this method.

Practice the same way (repeating one Bol or stroke over and over again). Also practice all the other Bols for Dayan and Bayan drums previously explained:

Note: The double bars || indicate unlimited repetition of the exercise.

EXAMPLE 15: EXERCISES FOR PRACTICE

TRACK 15 DISK 01

1 | Ta - Ta - Ta - Ta - Ta - ||

   | Te - Te - Te - Te - Te - ||

   ...

EXAMPLE 16: MORE EXERCISES

TRACK 16 DISK 01

2 | Ta - Ti - Ta - Tin - Ta - Ti - Ta - Tin - ||

3 | Ge - Ta - Ge - Ta - Ge - Ta - ||

4 | Ti - Ge - Ta - Ge - Ti - Ge - Ta - Ge - ||

5 | Ke - Ta - Ge - Ta - Ke - Ta - Ge - Ta - ||

6 | Ka - Ti - Ka - Tin - Ka - Ti - Ka - Tin - ||

7 | Kat - Ta - Kat - Ti - Kat - Tin - ||

8 | Dha - Na - Dha - Na - Dha - Na - ||

9 | Dha - Ti - Dha - Ti - Dha - Ti - ||

10 | Dha - Tin - Dha - Tin - Dha - Tin - ||

11 | Dha - Te - Dha - Te - Dha - Te - ||

12 | Dha - Tite - Dha - Tite - Dha - Tite - ||

EJERCICIOS DE PRÁCTICA

Los siguientes ejercicios tienen la intención de ayudar a desarrollar la habilidad técnica y la lectura en la ejecución de diferentes grupos de Bols. Comenzamos con frases simples y luego practicamos el resto de los ejercicios. Estos no son ciclos rítmicos o Talas, sino que son sólo ejemplos para práctica y entrenamiento. Los Talas se explicarán más adelante en este método.

Practicar de la misma manera, repitiendo una y otra vez; también practicar así cada uno de los Bols o golpes explicados anteriormente para Dayan y Bayan:

Nota: La doble barra || en cada ejercicio indica repetición sin limite.

EJEMPLO 15: EJERCICIOS DE PRÁCTICA

Dayan Bols / *Bols del Dayan* : **Ta, Te, Ti, Tin, Tite,** and **Tirikita**

Bayan Bols / *Bols del Bayan* : **Ge, Ke, Ka, Kat**

combined Bols / *Bols combinados* : **Dha, Dhe, Dhi, Dhin**

EJEMPLO 16: MÁS EJERCICIOS DE PRÁCTICA

13 | Dha - Tirikita - Dha - Tirikita - ||

14 | Dha - Ge - Dha - Ge - Dha - Ge - ||

15 | Dhe - Ge - Dhe - Ge - Dhe - Ge - ||

16 | Dhi - Ge - Dhi- Ge - Dhi - Ge - ||

17 | Dhin - Ge - Dhin - Ge - Dhin - Ge - ||

18 | Dha - Ge - Ta - Dha - Ge - Ta - ||

19 | Dha - Ge - Ta - Ti - Dha - Ge - Na - Ti - Dha - Ge - Ta - Ti - ||

20 | Dha - Dha - Dhe - Dhe - Dhi - Dhi - Dhin - Dhin - ||

21 | Dha - Dha - Tite - Dha - Dha - Tite - Dha - Dha - Tite - ||

Now, try to figure it out for yourself (without the CD's help), and practice the rest of the following exercises. It is suggested to recite the Bols out loud, in order to stimulate the auditive memory.

Ahora, tengan a bien continuar practicando el resto de los ejercicios sin la ayuda del CD. Se recomienda recitar en voz alta los Bols, para estimular la memoria auditiva.

22 | Dha - Dhe - Tite - Dha - Dhe - Tite - Dha - Dhe - Tite - ||

23 | Dha - Dhi - Tite - Dha - Dhi - Tite - Dha - Dhi - Tite - ||

24 | Dha - Ge - Tite - Dha - Ge - Tite - Dha - Ge - Tite - ||

25 | Ke - Ta - Ge - Ta - Ke - Ta - Ge - Ta - Ke - Ta - Ge - Ta - ||

26 | Ti - Ta - Ka - Ta - Ti - Ta - Ka - Ta - Ti - Ta - Ka - Ta - ||

27 | Ta - Ke - Dhi - Na - Ta - Ke - Dhi - Na - Ta - Ke - Dhi - Na - ||

28 | Ka - Ta - Dha - Tite - Ka - Ta - Dha - Tite - Ka - Ta - Dha - Tite - ||

29 | Ke - Na - Dha - Ti - Ke - Na - Dha - Ti - Ke - Na - Dha - Ti - ||

30 | Tite - Ka - Ta - Dha - Tite - Ka - Ta - Dha - Tite - Ka - Ta - Dha - ||

31 | Na - Dhi - Dhi - Na - Na - Dhi - Dhi - Na - Na - Dhi - Dhi - Na - ||

32 | Na - Dhi - Dhin - Na - Na - Dhi - Dhin - Na - Na - Dhi - Dhin - Na - ||

33 | Dha - Ge - Tirikita - Dha - Ge - Tirikita - Dha - Ge - Tirikita - ||

34 | Dha - Ge - Tite - Ka -Ta - Dha - Ge - Tite - Ka - Ta - ||

35 | Ka - Dhi - Ta - Dha - Ge - Na - Ka - Dhi - Ta - Dha - Ge - Na - ||

36 | Ta - Dha - Ge - Tite - Ka - Ta - Ke - Na - Dha - Ge - Tite - Ka -Ta - ||

37 | Dha - Tite - Ka - Ta - Dha - Ge - Ti - Na - Ge - Na - ||

38 | Dha - Dhi - Dhi - Dha - Ta - Tin - Tin - Ta - ||

39 | Ge - Na - Dha - Ge - Tirikita - Ge - Na - Dha - Ge - Tirikita - ||

40 | Ta - Ke - Dhin - Na - Ge - Na - Dha - Tirikita - Dha - Ge - Tirikita - ||

DEFINITION OF INDUSTANI RHYTHMIC TERMS

Matra: This is a basic measure of time – beat – used in the Industani music system of North India. A Matra does not have any specific length, but is designed according to the *Lay – tempo* or speed – (of the performance), that musicians suggest – or agree – as the appropiate one for that particular performance.

Nevertheless, there is an accepted standard of 1 second per Matra as a length for Medium Tempo, 2 seconds per Matra for Slow Tempo, and 1/2 second per Matra for Fast Tempo. Let's see the following graphic:

DEFINICIONES DE TÉRMINOS RÍTMICOS INDOSTÁNICOS

Matra: Un Matra es una unidad básica de medida de tiempo utilizado en la música Indostánica (sistema musical del norte de India). El Matra no tiene una duración específica o valor de tiempo, pero se fija de acuerdo al *Lay – tempo* o velocidad – que los músicos estipulen como apropiado para esa interpretación.

De todas maneras hay un estándar aceptado de 1 segundo por Matra de duración en velocidad media, 2 segundos por Matra en velocidad Lenta y 1/2 segundo por Matra o 2 Matras por segundo en velocidad rápida. Veamos el grafico que sigue:

Medium Tempo – Time (seconds) :	| <u>1 sec.</u> <u>2 sec.</u> <u>3 sec.</u> <u>4 sec.</u> |	*: Tiempo (segundos)* – **Tempo Medio**
Matra :	1 2 3 4	*: Matra*
Slow Tempo – Time (seconds) :	| <u>1 - 2 sec.</u> <u>3 - 4 sec.</u> <u>5 - 6 sec.</u> <u>7 - 8 sec.</u> |	*: Tiempo (segundos)* – **Tempo Lento**
Matra :	1 2 3 4	*: Matra*
Fast Tempo – Time (seconds) :	| <u>0.5 sec.</u> <u>1 sec.</u> <u>1.5 sec.</u> <u>2 sec.</u> |	*: Tiempo (segundos)* – **Tempo Rápido**
Matra :	1 2 3 4	*: Matra*

Lay: Means speed or tempo for each music performance or composition. As explained earlier, there are 3 standard Lay categories, described as follow:

Lay: Significa velocidad o tempo para cada interpretación o composición musical. Como explicado anteriormente, hay 3 categorías principales de Lay o velocidad, descritas a continuación:

VILAMBIT LAY: Slow tempo or speed. 2 seconds per Matra		**VILAMBIT LAY:** velocidad lenta. 1 Matra cada 2 segundos

VILAMBIT LAY: Slow tempo or speed. 2 seconds per Matra

MADHYA LAY: Medium tempo or speed, 1 second per Matra

DRUT LAY: Fast tempo or speed, 1/2 second per Matra

For any tempo or speed chosen, the Matra value remains constant.

In the examples depicted throughout this method, the time value of each Matra in relation to the pattern of Bols (or strokes) per second, is suggested using underlines. For example:

VILAMBIT LAY: velocidad lenta. 1 Matra cada 2 segundos

MADHYA LAY: velocidad media. 1 Matra cada 1 segundo

DRUT LAY: velocidad rápida. 1 Matra cada 1/2 segundo o 2 Matras por segundo.

Para cualquier tempo o velocidad adjudicado, el valor del Matra permanece constante.

En los ejemplos que se brindan en este método, el valor de tiempo de un Matra se indica en relación con el patrón de Bols o golpes, a través del subrayado. Algunos ejemplos:

EXAMPLE 17

EJEMPLO 17

TRACK 17 DISK 01

1 Bol per Matra : | Dha Dhi Dhi Dha | : 1 Bol por Matra
               1 2 3 4

2 Bols per Matra : | Dha Ge Ti Ge Na ge | : 2 Bols por Matra
               1   2   3

3 Bols per Matra : | Dhi Ta Ti Kat Ta Dha | : 3 Bols por Matra
               1   2

4 Bols per Matra : | Ti Ri Ki Ta Ti Te Ka Ta | : 4 Bols por Matra
               1   2

RHYTHMIC PHRASES WITH TWO, THREE, FOUR, SIX AND EIGHT MATRAS FOR PRACTICE

FRASES RÍTMICAS CON DOS, TRES, CUATRO, SEIS Y OCHO MATRAS PARA PRÁCTICA

The following exercises are composed of Matras or beats with several Bol patterns, for example: **DHA DHINA**. This phrase has 2 Matras (or beats), during which three Bols are played. Each Matra contains a different Bol pattern, indicated by underlining the Bols. The first Matra has only one Bol: **DHA**, while the second Matra has 2 Bols: **DHI** and **NA**.

If this phrase is going to be played in *Madhya Lay* or Medium Tempo (1 second per Matra, total: 2 seconds), then the first Matra has just 1 Bol **DHA** in the first second and the next Matra has 2 Bols which are **DHI** = 1/2 sec. and **NA** = 1/2 sec. Therefore, it could be said that within the first Matra, **DHA** is equivalent to one quarter-note or (♩) in the Western-style notation, while within the second Matra, **DHINA** is equivalent to two eighth-notes or (♪♪).

Los siguientes ejercicios están compuestos por Matras o tiempos, con diferentes patrones de Bols. Por ejemplo: **DHA DHINA**. Esta frase tiene 2 Matras (o tiempos), y en ella se tocan 3 Bols (o golpes) dentro de los 2 tiempos que se marcan con las líneas subrayadas. El primer Matra posee en sí un solo Bol: **DHA**, mientras que el segundo Matra está conformado por dos Bols: **DHI** y **NA**.

Si esta frase es tocada en *Madhya Lay* o velocidad media (1 segundo por Matra, en total: 2 segundos), entonces el primer Matra posee un solo Bol: **DHA**, con una duración de 1 segundo, mientras que el siguiente Matra posee dos Bols, a saber **DHI** – 1/2 seg. – y **NA** – 1/2 seg. Por lo tanto, se puede decir que dentro del primer Matra, **DHA** equivale a una negra (♩) en la notación musical occidental (o de pentagrama), mientras que dentro del segundo Matra, **DHINA** equivale a dos corcheas (♪♪).

♩   ♪   ♪
| Dha Dhi Na | 2 Matras
   1   2

This is the explanation about the relationship between a Matra and the different amount of Bols it could contain within itself.

De esta manera queda explicada la relación entre un Matra y la diferente cantidad de Bols que puede contener dentro de sí.

EXAMPLE 18

EJEMPLO 18

3 Matras

4 Matras

6 Matras

8 Matras

TALAS – RHYTHMIC CYCLES

In Indian music, the rhythmic organization is basically based in a structure of rhythmic cycles and patterns, which are continuously repeated during a music performance.

These cycles are called *Tal* or *Talas*. Each (Tal or) Tala has a fixed number of *Matras* or beats, and also a specific subdivision called *Vibhag(s)* or Bar(s). Within these Vibhags a specific number of Matras is placed.

Talas have a particular characteristic that is given by specific accents or stressed strokes, each of them placed throughout the different Vibhags. These accents also have a specific degree of importance inside the Tala structure: The main or principal accent is called *Sam*, the secondary accent is the *Khali*, and the minor accents are the *Tali*. We will refer to these topics again later in this method.

The first example of rhythmic cycle or Tala is the *Tin Tal*, the most popular in the Industani Rhythmic System. Tin Tal has a cyclic pattern with 16 Matras subdivided into 4 Vibhags containing 4 Matras each. See the graphic below:

TIN TAL

TALAS – CICLOS RÍTMICOS

En la música de la India, la organización rítmica se basa principalmente en una estructura subyacente de patrones y ciclos rítmicos que se repiten una y otra vez durante una interpretación musical.

Estos patrones rítmicos se denominan *Tal* o *Talas*. Cada Tala posee un número fijo de *Matras* o tiempos, y también una subdivisión específica llamada *Vibhag* o compás, dentro de la cual se incluye un número específico de Matras.

El patrón característico de un Tal en particular se distingue por el emplazamiento de acentos o golpes acentuados, ubicados a lo largo de los diferentes Vibhags. Estos acentos también tienen un determinado nivel de importancia dentro de la estructura de un Tala: El acento principal se denomina *Sam*, el secundario es el *Khali*, mientras que los menores son los *Tali*. Trataremos nuevamente estos tópicos más adelante en el método.

El primer ejemplo de ciclo rítmico o Tala es el *Tin Tal*, el más popular del Sistema Rítmico Indostánico. El Tin Tal tiene un patrón cíclico de 16 Matras, subdividido en 4 Vibhags que contienen 4 Matras cada uno.

TIN TAL

Matra (Beat) / *Matra (Tiempo)*   Vibhag (Bar) / *Vibhag (Compás)*

Matras: |① 2 3 4 | 5 6 7 8 | 9 10 11 12 | 13 14 15 16 |

Pattern of **Tala** (rhythmic cycle) **Tin Tal**
*Patrón del **Tala** (ciclo rítmico) **Tin Tal***

Taking the example of the rhythmic cycle called Tin Tal, this pattern has 4 divisions or Vibhags with 4 Matras each, a total of 16 Matras: 4 + 4 + 4 + 4. Therefore, when a composition is performed in Tin Tal, it has two similar phrases with 8 Matras each. These phrases complement each other in a sense that the first one has all resonant Bols in it, while the second phrase substitute its first half with non-resonant Bols.

Tomando el ejemplo del ciclo rítmico denominado Tin Tal, el patrón cíclico de 16 Matras está dividido en 4 partes iguales o 4 Vibhags de 4 Matras cada uno, o sea 16 Matras: 4 + 4 + 4 + 4. Por lo tanto, cuando una composición es interpretada en Tin Tal, se presenta en 2 frases similares de 8 Matras cada una. Estas frases se complementan unas con otras en el sentido de que la primera frase se compone de golpes resonantes, mientras que la segunda sustituye por golpes no resonantes la primera mitad de su frase.

These particular characteristics in the rhythmic cycle's structure are very important, in order to understand the Indian Talas; it's precisely because of them – this uniqueness (there is no other music system in the world that has these characteristics) –, and its profound meaning that it has been called 'rhythmic poetry', from both the artistic and the aesthetic perspective.

At this point it's good to notice that the rhythms in Indian music have a kind of 'breathing', a rhythmical inhaling and exhaling, precisely because of the interaction of the resonant and non-resonant Bols or strokes, the respectively main and empty Vibhags and accents like Sam and Khali.

Estas características particulares que presenta la estructura de un ciclo rítmico son muy importantes para poder comprender los Talas. Es precisamente por esto que es único (no existe en todo el mundo un sistema de estas características), y por su profundo significado, que se le denomina 'Poesía Rítmica', tanto desde la perspectiva artística como desde la estética.

A esta altura, es bueno resaltar que los ritmos en la música de la India tienen una especie de respiración, un rítmico inhalar y exhalar, precisamente por la interacción de los Bols resonantes con los no resonantes, así como por los respectivos Vibhags o compases y acentos principales y vacíos, como el Sam y el Khali.

KEEPING TALA

Every musician in India keeps control of the Tala because of this form of measurment – 'Keeping Tala'. Instead of counting the beats or Matras, they focus on the Bars or Vibhags, and when the *Khali Vibhag* or empty bar arrives, they can understand exactly where they are in the Tala or rhythmic cycle.

The following example shows the different accents, its symbols, and where they are placed throughout the different bars of the Tin Tal rhythmic cycle. Follow the Theka Tal by listening to the accents.

SOLFEO RÍTMICO DE UN TALA

Los músicos en la India toman control de un Tal gracias a esta forma de solfeo. En lugar de contar los Matras, ellos se enfocan en los Vibhags, y cuando aparece un *Khali Vibhag*, o compás vacío, entienden exactamente en que parte del Tala se encuentran.

El siguiente ejemplo muestra los distintos acentos, sus símbolos, y dónde se ubican dentro de cada compás en el ciclo rítmico Tin Tal. Seguir el Theka Tal guiándose por los acentos

EXAMPLE 19

EJEMPLO 19

| | Accents | | Empty accent | |
| | *Acentos* | | *Acento vacío* | |

| sam | tali | khali | tali |
| + | – | o | – |

Dha dhi dhi dha | dha dhi dhi dha | dha tin tin ta | ta dhi dhi dha |

1　2　3　4　　5　6　7　8　　9　10　11　12　　13　14　15　16

| Sam vibhag | Tali vibhag | Khali vibhag | Tali vibhag |

| 1st Phrase | 2nd Phrase |
| *Frase 1* | *Frase 2* |

+

SAM: This accent is the main or principal accent of the Tala. The Bol stressed with Sam is played louder than all the rest. It marks the beginning of a Tala. A strong hand-clap is used to mark this accent during the 'Keeping Tala'.

+

SAM: Este acento marca el comienzo de un Tal y es su acento principal. El Bol marcado por el Sam se toca más fuerte que los demás. En el solfeo rítmico el Sam se marca con una fuerte palmada.

o

KHALI: This accent is the second in importance after the Sam. It literally means 'empty', and the entire Bar that has a Khali accent should be played softly and without any resonant Bols. A wave with the hand is used to mark the Khali accent.

o

KHALI: Es el acento secundario de un Tal. Significa literalmente 'vacío', y todo el compás debe ser tocado más suave y sin Bols resonantes. En el solfeo rítmico el Khali se marca con un movimiento ondulante de la mano, sin realizar sonido alguno.

TALI: This accent is called 'minor', and is the least important. The Bol stressed with Tali should be played a little louder than the others, but less than the Sam. Tali also means 'clap', and one handclap is used to mark each Tali accent.

All these symbols have an important role in the counting sequence of the Tala. This counting should be made along with hands and fingers, clapping and waving gestures with the entire hand for each Vibhag, plus finger counting the Beats or Matras of the Tala. These hand movements are tools to develop what is currently known as 'Keeping Tala'.

TALI: Este acento es llamado menor, y es el menos importante. El Bol marcado con el Tali se debe tocar un poco más fuerte que los demás, pero menos que el Sam. Tali también significa 'palmada', por lo que una palmada suave se usa en el solfeo rítmico para marcarlo.

Todos estos símbolos tienen un rol muy importante en el conteo secuencial de un Tala. Este conteo debe hacerse con manos y dedos en cada Vibhag, aplaudiendo y con gestos de silencio, además de contar cada tiempo o Matra del Tala. Estos movimientos sirven de herramientas para el desarrollo de lo que se denomina 'solfeo rítmico de un Tala'.

COUNTING THE TALA

EXAMPLE 20: FINGER COUNT – FIRST VERSION

CONTEO DE UN TALA

EJEMPLO 20: CONTEO CON LOS DEDOS – PRIMERA VERSIÓN

TRACK
20
DISK
01

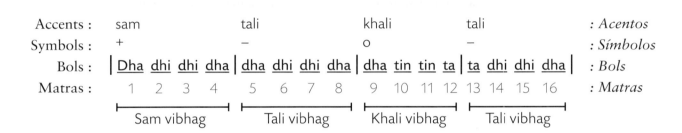

Accents :	sam				tali				khali				tali				: *Acentos*
Symbols :	+				–				o				–				: *Símbolos*
Bols :	Dha	dhi	dhi	dha	dha	dhi	dhi	dha	dha	tin	tin	ta	ta	dhi	dhi	dha	: *Bols*
Matras :	1	2	3	4	5	6	7	8	9	10	11	12	13	14	15	16	: *Matras*

Sam vibhag   Tali vibhag   Khali vibhag   Tali vibhag

1
2

1 & 2: Start the solfege by clapping on the first beat or **Sam**;

*Comenzar el solfeo rítmico dando una palmada en el primer acento o **Sam**;*

3
4

3, 4 & 5: Then, continue with the finger count, starting with the *little finger* and followed by the *ring* and *middle* fingers on the 2nd, 3rd and 4th beat of the **Tin Tala** respectively. Repeat this counting during the second bar too;

*Continuar contando los tiempos subsiguientes con los dedos meñique, anular y medio en el segundo, tercero y cuarto tiempo del **Tin Tala** respectivamente. Repetir durante el segundo compás;*

5

6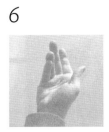

6: When the **Khali** accent arrives, it's time to do the *'wave'* gesture with the hand, that marks the *empty accent* that exists within every rhythmic cycle in Indian music. After the *'Wave'* on the third bar is done, it comes back to the finger count again as usual, counting the fourth bar in the same way as the first two.

Al llegar al **Khali** *o acento vacío, realizar el gesto sin sonido que denota 'vacío' abriendo el dorso de la mano con la palma hacia arriba; luego continuar el cuarto compás solfeando con los dedos y palmadas como en el primero y segundo compás.*

To understand a Tala in the Industani music system, it is necessary to use the 'finger count' system to keep track of the Matras or beats, in order to recognize in which part of the Tala one is located.

Sam (+) and Tali (–) accents are counted by hand claps, while the Khali (o) or empty accent is counted either by waving the preferred hand in the air, or clapping with the 'back' of one hand, instead of the usual handclap.

KEEPING TALA: Start by reciting with the voice each Bol of the Tala, for example the *Tin Tal* in *Madhya Lay* or Medium Tempo – 1 second per Matra. At the same time in order to know in which Vibhag one is located, clap each Sam and Tali accents, and then clap with the back of the hand or make a wave movement without any sound when the Khali accent comes on the way. The remaining Matras are counted with the little, ring and middle fingers respectively.

Para poder comprender un Tal en el sistema de aprendizaje de la música Indostánica, es necesario utilizar el sistema de conteo de dedos para indicar Matras y así reconocer en qué parte del Tal uno se encuentra.

Las palmadas son para los acentos Sam (+), y Tali (–), mientras que para el Khali (o) se utiliza un gesto curvo al aire, o una palmada sin sonido utilizando el dorso de la mano en lugar de la palmada usual de los demás acentos.

SOLFEO RÍTMICO DE UN TALA: Comenzar recitando en voz alta cada Bol de un Tal; en este caso solfearemos el *Tin Tal* a velocidad media – *Madhya Lay*: 1 segundo por Matra. Al mismo tiempo, y con el fin de recordar en que Vibhag uno se encuentra, palmear cada acento Sam y Tali. Luego palmear con el dorso de la mano o hacer el gesto curvo en el aire cuando aparece el acento Khali. El resto de los Matras se marca contando con los dedos meñique, anular y medio sucesivamente.

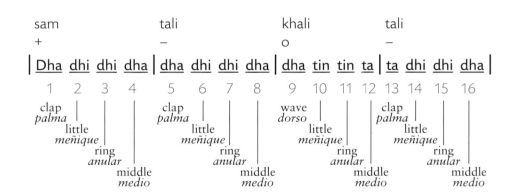

Remember that in the Tin Tala, the third Vibhag is Khali, without resonant Bols:

Recordar que en el Tin Tala, el tercer Vibhag es Khali, o sea sin Bols resonantes:

| sam | tali | khali | tali |
| + | – | o | – |

| Dha dhi dhi dha | dha dhi dhi dha | dha **tin tin ta** | **ta** dhi dhi dha |

non-resonant Bols
Bols no resonantes

FINGER COUNT – SECOND VERSION

There is another way of 'finger counting' the Talas, that is very popular among the musicians in India. It works by counting with each finger's phalange as shown bellow:

CONTEO CON LOS DEDOS – SEGUNDA VERSIÓN

Existe otra forma muy popular entre los musicos en India de 'solfeo rítmico' de Talas, que se realiza contando con las falanges de cada dedo de la mano:

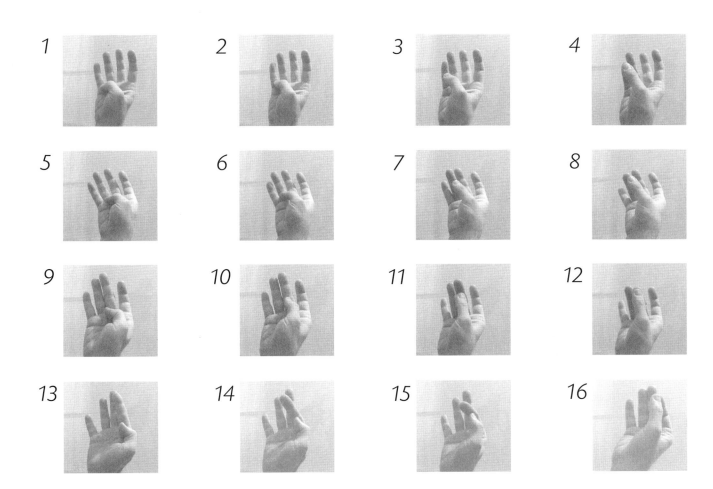

FIXED COMPOSITION BASED ON THE TIN TAL
– 16 BEATS –

COMPOSICIÓN FIJA BASADA EN EL 'TIN TAL'
– 16 TIEMPOS –

It is time now to start with the *Fixed Compositions*. At this point it is essential to have memorized and practiced all the information we have explained earlier in this method, otherwise it will be almost impossible to understand the following section.

Here is an example of a theme of the *Kaida 1* that has been composed in *Tin Tal*. You can also see it later on this method, in the *Kaidas* section, CHAPTER III.

Ha llegado el momento de comenzar con el tema: *Composiciones Fijas*. A esta altura del método es esencial haber memorizado y practicado toda la información anteriormente explicada; de otra manera les será casi imposible entender la siguiente sección.

El siguiente es un ejemplo de un tema del *Kaida 1* que ha sido compuesto en *Tin Tal*, y también se encuentra más adelante en el CAPÍTULO III: *Kaidas*.

EXAMPLE 21

EJEMPLO 21

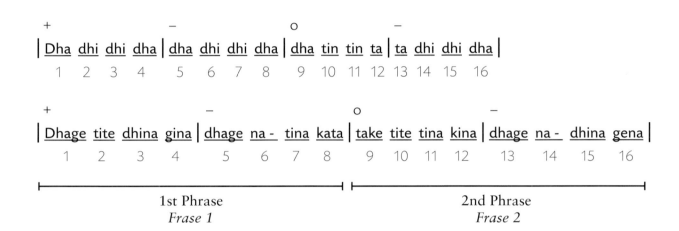

+					–			o				–			
Dha	dhi	dhi	dha	dha	dhi	dhi	dha	dha	tin	tin	ta	ta	dhi	dhi	dha
1	2	3	4	5	6	7	8	9	10	11	12	13	14	15	16

+				–				o				–			
Dhage	tite	dhina	gina	dhage	na -	tina	kata	take	tite	tina	kina	dhage	na -	dhina	gena
1	2	3	4	5	6	7	8	9	10	11	12	13	14	15	16

1st Phrase
Frase 1

2nd Phrase
Frase 2

In the Tabla set, the resonance section is produced by the Bol **GE** on the *Bayan* drum, either by itself or combined with other *Dayan* Bols, for example: **DHA**, is **TA** + **GE**. When the non-resonant Bols appear in the *Khali Vibhag*, it substitutes the sound **GE** with the **KE** (when just a **GE**), or omits it altogether, playing only non-resonant Bols; for example, **DHA** changes to just **TA**.

In this example, the resonant phrase '**DHAGE** – **TITE** – **DHINA** – **GINA**', that appears in the first Vibhag of the composition, has been replaced in the Khali Vibhag by non-resonant '**TAKE** – **TITE** – **TINA** – **KINA**', that is its complementary phrase. After this, the composition continues without further modifications.

En el Tabla, la resonancia se produce con el **GE** del *Bayan*, solo o combinado con otro golpe del *Dayan*, por ejemplo: **DHA** : **TA** + **GE**. Los Bols no resonantes que aparecen en el *Khali Vibhag* sustituyen al Bol resonante **GE**, por **KE** (en el caso de ser **GE** solo), o lo omiten por completo en el caso de ser un Bol combinado; por ejemplo: **DHA** cambia a **TA**.

En este ejemplo, la frase resonante '**DHAGE** – **TITE** – **DHINA** – **GINA**' que aparece en el primer Vibhag, es reemplazada en el Khali Vibhag por los Bols no resonantes '**TAKE** – **TITE** – **TINA** – **KINA**', que forman su frase complementaria. Luego la composición continúa sin modificaciones.

EXAMPLE 22

EJEMPLO 22

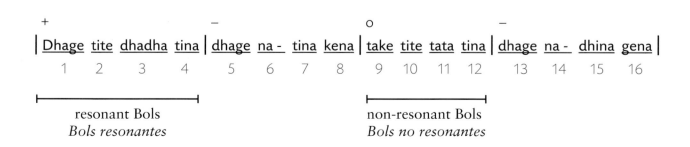

+				–				o				–			
Dhage	tite	dhadha	tina	dhage	na -	tina	kena	take	tite	tata	tina	dhage	na -	dhina	gena
1	2	3	4	5	6	7	8	9	10	11	12	13	14	15	16

resonant Bols
Bols resonantes

non-resonant Bols
Bols no resonantes

This alternating between resonant and non-resonant Vibhags and Bols (bars and strokes respectively) produces a sonority distinction. It means that the Bols are open, expanded and full of sound in the Sam and Tali Vibhags, as opposed to the contracted and empty Bols of the Khali Vibhag.

This procedure, which defines the structural form of a rhythmic cycle or *Tal* applies to all the examples of *Kaidas* (fixed compositions) and variations which are shown in this method. This is how we can perceive the breathing effect, which takes place with the interaction of the Sam, Khali and Tali accents and bars.

Note: Please make it a rule to use first vocal recitation and finger counting in every example given throughout this method, and then go ahead using the Tabla set. This helps a lot to memorize the Bols and examples 'by ear', as taught by the Masters in ancient times.

For example: Let us imagine that in the beginning of the Tala or rhythmic cycle, the Sam accent has the '*inhaling*' effect of the rhythm, and when the Khali accent arrives in the middle of the Tala, the '*exhaling*' effect takes place, all the way until the Sam comes once again, in the same way of the breathing cycle.

TIN TAL – 16 MATRAS:

Esta alternancia entre Vibhags y Bols resonantes y no-resonantes produce una distinción de sonoridades. Esto significa que los Bols son abiertos, expandidos y llenos de sonido en el Sam y Tali Vibhags, y se oponen a las sonoridades vacías y contraídas del Khali Vibhag.

Este procedimiento define la forma estructural de un ciclo rítmico o *Tal* y es aplicable a todos los ejemplos de *Kaida* (composiciones fijas) y variaciones que veremos en este método. De esta manera es posible apreciar como los Talas o ciclos rítmicos pueden 'respirar' mediante la interacción de sus acentos Sam, Khali y Tali, junto con los Vibhags o compases que los contienen.

Nota: Volver una regla el recitar y solfear en voz alta cada ejemplo dado en este método; luego tocarlo en el Tabla. Esto ayuda mucho a memorizar los Bols y ejercicios 'de oído', además de ser la forma en que los Maestros enseñaban en la antigüedad.

Por ejemplo: Es posible imaginar que al comenzar el Tala o ciclo rítmico el Sam podría ser la '*inhalación*' del ritmo; y cuando aparece el Khali o acento vacío en la mitad del ciclo, comienza la '*exhalación*' del ritmo hasta que llega nuevamente al Sam y comienza de nuevo, del mismo modo que un ciclo de respiración.

TIN TAL – 16 MATRAS:

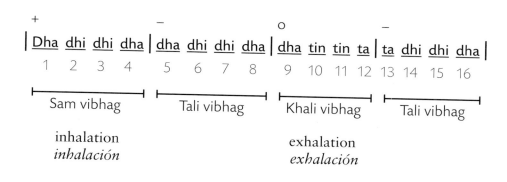

It is important to observe that there are other kinds of compositions in Indian music that do not follow these procedures, like the *Tihai* or ending (which will be analyzed later). There are also other composition forms like the *Chakradar Gat, Tipalli, Tukra, Amad*, among others.

Es importante observar que otras composiciones en la música India – como el *Tihai* que se analizará luego – no siguen este proceder. Existen además otras formas de composición para Tabla, como el *Chakradar Gat, Tipalli, Tukra, Amad*, entre otras.

The following list has some basic resonant / non-resonant Bols substitutions, that are commonly used during the Khali Vibhag:

La siguiente lista contiene algunas sustituciones de Bols resonantes por Bols no resonantes que se utilizan comunmente en el Khali Vibhag:

EXAMPLE 23

EJEMPLO 23

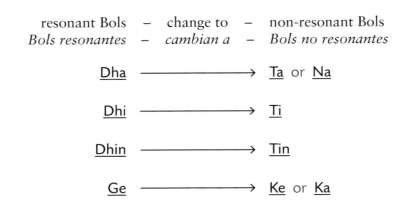

resonant Bols	– change to –	non-resonant Bols
Bols resonantes	*– cambian a –*	*Bols no resonantes*

Dha ⟶ Ta or Na

Dhi ⟶ Ti

Dhin ⟶ Tin

Ge ⟶ Ke or Ka

KAIDA
Indo-Persian word that means 'Law' or 'Code'

KAIDA
Palabra de origen Indo–Persa que significa 'Ley' o 'Código'

A *Kaida* is a previously written composition. It is based on a particular Tala or rhythmic cycle as its basic metric platform, and is used by musicians as a basic source material for developing improvisations as well as creating other rhythmic compositions.

There are hundreds of Kaidas written in different *Gharanas* or styles, which have been orally passed from generation to generation of teacher/disciples to this day; and a variety of Bols, related to the different techniques that has been developed by each Gharana.

Note: Most of the following CD Examples start with 2 or more Theka cycles (for example Tin Tal). This is helpful to give the form and tempo of the piece.

The development of a Kaida has three different sections:
1. Main Theme or **Kaida**
2. **Variations** of a Kaida
3. **Tihai** or end.

Un *Kaida* es una composición escrita previamente. Posee un Tal como base métrica, y es una fuente de material básico que el músico posteriormente desarrolla y transforma en improvisación u otras frases rítmicas.

Existen cientos de Kaidas escritos en diferentes estilos y variedad de *Gharanas*, los cuales han sido transmitidos oralmente por generaciones de maestros/discípulos hasta nuestros días, además de una diversa variedad de Bols relacionados con las diferentes técnicas que han sido desarrolladas por cada Gharana.

Nota: La mayoría de los Ejemplos de Audio que siguen a continuación comienzan con 2 o más ciclos del Theka respectivo (por ejemplo Tin Tal). Con ello se da la forma y la velocidad de la interpretación.

El desarrollo de un Kaida consta de 3 secciones diferentes:
1. Tema principal o **Kaida**
2. **Variaciones**
3. **Tihai** o final

1. MAIN THEME OR KAIDA:
The following is the same example of the Kaida 1 in *Tin Tal*, that was shown earlier in this method.

1. TEMA PRINCIPAL O KAIDA:
El siguiente es el ejemplo del Kaida 1 basado en *Tin Tal*, que ya hemos visto anteriormente en éste método.

EXAMPLE 24   **EJEMPLO 24**

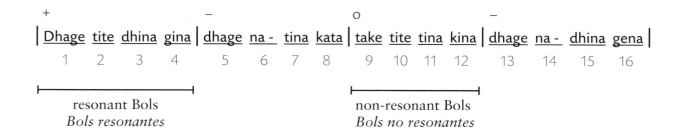

A Kaida is always performed in 2 rhythmic phrases, which complement each other with its resonant – non-resonant forms, as previously explained.

We have more Kaidas to learn and practice, also based on several Talas with its variations and Tihai, that will be shown later in the CHAPTER III of *Tabla for All*.

Una composición de Kaida basada en Tin Tal se presenta siempre en 2 frases iguales que se complementan entre sí en sus formas resonantes y no resonantes como ha sido explicado anteriormente.

Hay muchos otros Kaidas para aprender y practicar, también basados en distintos Talas, con sus variaciones y Tihai. Estos serán tratados más adelante, en el CAPÍTULO III de *Tabla para Todos*.

2. VARIATIONS:

These are the development section of a Kaida composition. It uses the same bols or strokes as the main Theme, but reorganized in a different way. This procedure does not change the resonant / non-resonant 2-phrase structure of a Kaida, that is kept the same throughout the entire composition.

Regarding variation structure, notice that, especially on Variations and Tihai, it expands the amount of Vibhags and Tali accents, with a duration of 2, 3, 4, etc. Tal Thekas. For this reason, the Khali Vibhag automatically displaces itself to the half part of any variation.

This explains why a Tala or Tal Theka doesn't necessarily need to have the same accents as a variation. Here is an example taken from the Kaida 1 in Tin Tal:

2. VARIACIONES:

Las variaciones son el desarrollo de un Kaida. Se utilizan los mismos bols que lleva su Tema principal, pero reagrupados de diferente manera. Este procedimiento no modifica la estructura de dos frases resonante / no resonante del Kaida, que continúa a través de toda la composición.

Refiriendo a la estructura de una variación, notar que, especialmente en Variaciones y Tihai, la cantidad de Vibhags y acentos Tali se expande generalmente a 2, 3, 4, etc. Tal Thekas. Por esta razón, el Khali Vibhag se desplaza automáticamente hacia la mitad de la variación.

Esto explica el por qué un Tala o Tal Theka no necesariamente tiene la misma acentuación que una variación. El siguiente es un ejemplo tomado del Kaida 1 en Tin Tal:

EXAMPLE 25   **EJEMPLO 25**

Variation | *Variación*

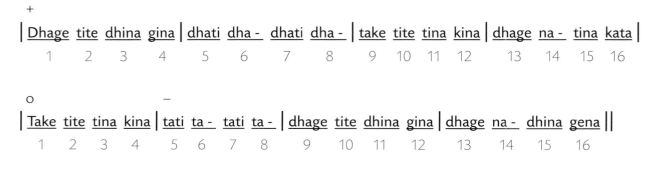

There is an alternative approach of a Variation performance that goes as follow:

The 2 resonant / non-resonant phrases structure of the Kaida is preserved in such a way, that the Variation presented can be played twice at double the speed – *Drut Lay*:

- First as a *full resonant* rhythmic phrase, and
- Second, followed by a *complementary form*, with non-resonant bols in the Khali Vibhag, or the first part of the second phrase.

EXAMPLE 26

Existe tambien una manera alternativa de tocar una variacion, que es la siguiente:

La estructura de 2 frases resonante / no resonante de un Kaida se mantiene de forma tal, que la variacion presentada puede ser tocada 2 veces y al doble de velocidad – *Drut Lay*:

- Primero como una frase *resonante completa*, y
- Segundo, seguido por su *forma complementaria*, con Bols no resonantes en el Khali Vibhag, o en la primera parte de la segunda frase.

EJEMPLO 26

Tin Tal

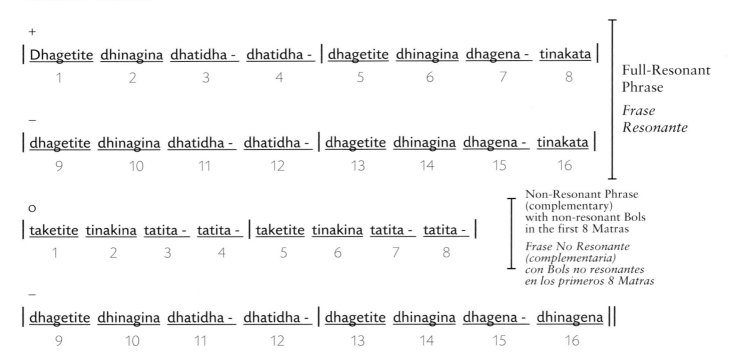

Variation | *Variación*

Another option for variations is that it could be performed at twice the original speed that the Kaida was originally composed.

However, it's not a necessary condition to apply in every Variation performed, but is generally used by musicians as part of their improvisational skills. For example:

Otra característica en muchas de las variaciones es que los patrones rítmicos pueden ser interpretados al doble de la velocidad original en que se creó el Kaida.

Esto, sin embargo, no es necesariamente aplicable a todas las variaciones, pero es una forma común que los músicos adoptan como parte de sus habilidades de improvisación. Por ejemplo:

EXAMPLE 27   **EJEMPLO 27**

TRACK 27 DISK 01

Variation | *Variación*

\+   –

| Dhagetite dhinagina dhatidha - dhatidha - | dhagetite dhinagina dhagena - tinakata |

    1   2   3   4   5   6   7   8

o   –

| taketite tinakina tatita - tatita - | dhagetite dhinagina dhagena - dhinagena ||

   9   10   11   12   13   14   15   16

Another example: if one Kaida is composed in Vilambit Lay – slow tempo –, then its variations could be performed at twice its original speed – Madhya Lay or medium tempo. But if one Kaida is composed in Drut Lay – fast tempo –, then its speed could not be duplicated, like in this Tin Tal example:

Otro ejemplo: si un Kaida está compuesto en Vilambit Lay o tiempo lento, sus variaciones se pueden tocar también doblando su Lay, o sea en Madhya. Pero si un Kaida esta compuesto en Drut Lay o tiempo rápido, éste no podrá ser tocado al doble, como en este ejemplo en Tin Tal:

EXAMPLE 28: KAIDA THEME IN DRUT LAY OR FAST SPEED

EJEMPLO 28: TEMA DEL KAIDA EN DRUT LAY O VELOCIDAD RÁPIDA

TRACK 28 DISK 01

Tin Tal

\+   –   o   –

| Dha dhi dhi dha | dha dhi dhi dha | dha tin tin ta | ta dhi dhi dha |

  1   2   3   4   5   6   7   8   9   10   11   12   13   14   15   16

Kaida Theme in **Drut Lay** | *Tema de Kaida en* **Drut Lay**

\+   –

| Dhagetite dhinagina dhagena - tinakata | dhagetite tinakina dhagena - dhinagena |

    1   2   3   4   5   6   7   8

1st Phrase – Full-Resonant
Frase 1 – Resonante

o   –

| (taketite tinakina takena - tinakata) | dhagetite dhinagina dhagena - dhinagena |

   9   10   11   12   13   14   15   16

2nd Phrase – Non-Resonant (complementary) with non-resonant Bols in the first 4 Matras
Frase 2 – No Resonante (complementaria) con Bols no resonantes en los primeros 4 Matras

REPETITION OF RHYTHMIC PHRASES

In this method, the repetition of rhythmic phrases inside Kaida variations or other compositions are written using *Brackets* and *Parenthesis* symbols. These useful tools are used to indicate that every phrase inside Brackets and Parenthesis should be repeated as much times as indicated by the number located above each symbol.

This example is a Variation of the *Kaida 1* in Tin Tal, that is shown later on the Kaidas' practice section in CHAPTER III.

EXAMPLE 29

REPETICIÓN DE FRASES

A lo largo de este método, la repetición de frases rítmicas dentro de las variaciones de un Kaida u otras composiciones, están escritas utilizando los símbolos de *Corchetes* y *Paréntesis*. Estos son herramientas útiles para indicar que cada frase escrita dentro de ellos debe repetirse tantas veces como lo requiera el numero ubicado sobre ellos.

Este ejemplo es una variación del *Kaida 1* en Tin Tal, que se desarrolla luego en la sección practica de Kaidas, CAPÍTULO III.

EJEMPLO 29

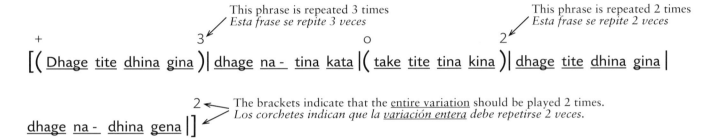

PAUSE OR REST

Pauses are indicated by a *dash* (-), and are used to show that in one particular space in the composition there is a pause or silence with no sound or Bol.

EXAMPLE 30

The following are some examples of how a pause or rest is used in a composition:

1. **- DHA**: In this case, the Matra or beat has two parts (indicated by the *underline*): one is a pause (dash) that lasts 1/2 a Matra, and the other is the Bol **DHA**, that lasts the other 1/2 of a Matra, or *eighth* note in western music notation.

Here goes an example in Tin Tal – 16 beats cycle:

PAUSA O SILENCIO

Las pausas se indican con un *guión* (-). Estos sirven para indicar que en un espacio en particular dentro de una composición existe un silencio o pausa sin sonido o Bol.

EJEMPLO 30

Los siguientes son algunos ejemplos del uso de una pausa en una composición:

1. **- DHA**: Indica que el Matra se divide en 2 partes (indicado por el subrayado): El guión que marca la pausa y el Bol **DHA**, que dura 1/2 tiempo y la pausa otro 1/2 tiempo, equivalente a una corchea en el sistema de notación occidental.

Ver el siguiente ejemplo en Tin Tal de 16 tiempos:

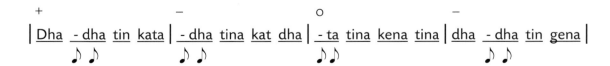

2. **DHA - NA**: Here the Matra has three parts; a pause or rest in between the Bols **DHA** and **NA**. Each one of them lasts 1/3 of a Matra, or a triplet in western notation.

2. **DHA - NA**: Indica que el Matra se divide en 3 partes, con una pausa o silencio entre los Bols **DHA** y **NA**. Cada Bol – al igual que la pausa – dura 1/3 del Matra, equivalente a un tresillo en notación occidental.

See this example in *Kherwa Tal* – 8 beats cycle:

```
        +           –        o           –
  | Dhite dha - na dhite tite | tite ta - na dhite tite |
         ⌐3⌐                      ⌐3⌐
```

3. DHA - TINA: In this example the Matra has four parts, DHA – *Pause* – TI – NA, each one of them lasts 1/4 of a Matra (sixteenth note).

See this example in *Dadra Tal* – 6 beats cycle:

```
        +                    o
  | Dha - tina dhi dhin | ta - tina dhi dhin |
```

Este ejemplo esta compuesto en *Kherwa Tal* de 8 tiempos.

3. DHA - TINA: indica que el Matra se divide en 4 partes iguales, DHA – *Pausa* – TI – NA. O sea que cada golpe y la pausa duran 1/4 de tiempo (semicorchea).

Este ejemplo esta en *Dadra Tal* de 6 tiempos:

TIHAI

The name *Tihai* refers to the conclusion or end of a section or composition. It's usually composed using the same Bols or strokes of the composition it belongs to. A Tihai may lead an entire composition to its end, but other Tihai forms simply indicate a transition from one part to another of the same composition.

The basic structure of a Tihai consists in one rhythmic phrase that is repeated three consecutive times, but in such a way that the last Bol or stroke of the last repeated phrase falls at the *Sam* (+), or first Bol of the next cycle; then the Tala continues – except if it marks the end of a composition – meaning that the Tala comes after the Tihai has been played.

This procedure is a particular feature of the Industani rhythmic system, because in the vast majority of the music we listen to, the end of a musical piece is always at the last beat of the bar. But in Indian music it is always at the first beat or Matra of a Tala.

The following are three different examples – out of many others, of a Tihai composition:

DUMDAR OR SIMPLE TIHAI: This Tihai form consists in one rhythmic phrase, that must be repeated 3 times, with a pause (-) located in between each phrase that lasts 1 Matra or beat. This Tihai is contained in 1 full cycle of 16 beats, plus 1 more beat that belongs to the next Tin Tal cycle – Sam (+). That means, a total of 17 beats.

In this example, the phrase is:

DHA TINA GADHI GINA DHA

Notice that the Bols GA and GI are different names for the same Bol GE.

TIHAI

Un *Tihai* marca la conclusión o final de una composición. Está usualmente integrado por los mismos Bols que posee un Kaida y lleva a su conclusión a la composición entera, aunque hay otras formas de Tihai que sólo indican el paso hacia otro movimiento dentro de una misma obra.

La estructura básica de un Tihai consiste en la repetición de una frase 3 veces sucesivas, pero de forma tal que el último Bol de la última frase repetida corresponde al *Sam* (+) o primer Bol del siguiente ciclo; luego el Tala continua – excepto en el caso de un final completo de una obra – o sea que el Tala sucede al Tihai, cuando éste finaliza.

Este procedimiento es una particularidad destacada en el sistema rítmico Indostánico. En la mayor parte de la música que escuchamos, el final de las composiciones es siempre en el ultimo tiempo del compás. Pero en música de la India, se finaliza siempre con el primer tiempo o Matra de un Tala.

Los siguientes son 3 ejemplos diferentes – entre tantos otros, de Tihai:

TIHAI SIMPLE O DUMDAR TIHAI: Esta forma de Tihai consiste en una frase rítmica que debe repetirse 3 veces, y con una pausa (-) ubicada entre cada frase que dura 1 Matra. Este Tihai está contenido en una vuelta completa del ciclo rítmico de 16 tiempos, más otro tiempo que coincide con el Sam (+) del Tal siguiente; o sea un total de 17 tiempos.

En este ejemplo la frase clave del Tihai es:

DHA TINA GADHI GINA DHA

Notar que los nombres de los Bols GA y GI son sinónimos del Bol GE.

EXAMPLE 31   EJEMPLO 31

Tin Tal – 16 Matras

```
      +                    –                    o                    –
   | Dha dhi dhi dha | dha dhi dhi dha | dha tin tin ta | ta dhi dhi dha |
      1   2   3   4     5   6   7   8     9  10  11 12   13  14  15  16
```

Dumdar Tihai

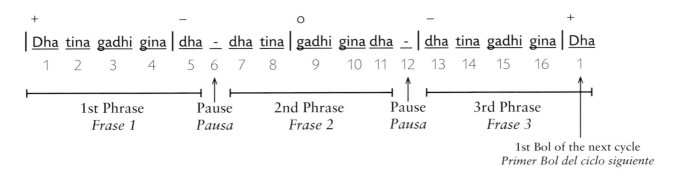

```
       +                      –                    o                      –                      +
   | Dha tina gadhi gina | dha - dha tina | gadhi gina dha - | dha tina gadhi gina | Dha
     1    2    3    4      5  6   7    8     9     10   11 12   13   14   15   16     1
```

|----------------------|---------|----------------------|---------|----------------------|

        1st Phrase   Pause   2nd Phrase   Pause   3rd Phrase
        Frase 1   *Pausa*   *Frase 2*   *Pausa*   *Frase 3*

                                                                   1st Bol of the next cycle
                                                                   Primer Bol del ciclo siguiente

BEDAM TIHAI: This Tihai form has one phrase that is repeated 3 times, but unlike the Dumdar, it does not include any pauses in between the phrases. It is also contained in 1 full cycle of 16 beats, plus 1 more beat that belongs to the next Tin Tal cycle.

In this example the phrase is:

DHINA DHA TINA GADHI GINA DHA

EXAMPLE 32

BEDAM TIHAI: Esta forma de Tihai posee una frase que se repite 3 veces, pero a diferencia del Dumdar Tihai, no incluye pausas entre frases. Igualmente, se encuentra contenido en un ciclo completo de 16 tiempos, al que se le agrega un tiempo que corresponde con el siguiente ciclo de Tin Tal.

En este ejemplo la frase clave del Tihai es:

DHINA DHA TINA GADHI GINA DHA

EJEMPLO 32

Tin Tal – 16 Matras

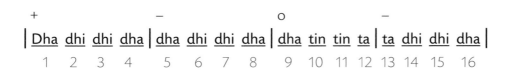

```
      +                    –                    o                    –
   | Dha dhi dhi dha | dha dhi dhi dha | dha tin tin ta | ta dhi dhi dha |
      1   2   3   4     5   6   7   8     9  10  11 12   13  14  15  16
```

Bedam Tihai

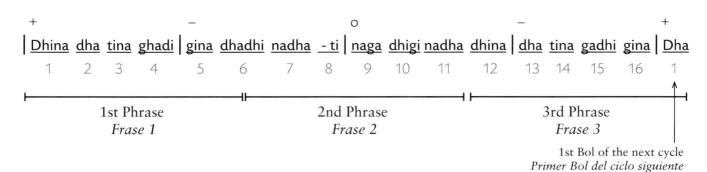

```
       +                        –                          o                        –                        +
   | Dhina dha tina ghadi | gina dhadhi nadha - ti | naga dhigi nadha dhina | dha tina gadhi gina | Dha
      1    2    3    4       5    6      7     8      9    10    11    12      13   14   15   16     1
```

|------------------------------|------------------------------|------------------------------|

            1st Phrase   2nd Phrase   3rd Phrase
            Frase 1   *Frase 2*   *Frase 3*

                                                                   1st Bol of the next cycle
                                                                   Primer Bol del ciclo siguiente

CHAKRADAR TIHAI: The Sanskrit word *Chakra* means 'wheel' or 'spin', therefore Chakradar could be translated as 'spin over spin,' or 'Spinning Tihai'. This is the purpose of the Chakradar Tihai, and it indicates the conclusion of an entire performance or composition.

This particular example of a Chakradar Tihai consists of one rhythmic phrase that is repeated 3 times, with a pause in between them that lasts half a Matra, and at the same time these 3 phrases are repeated 3 times in its entirety.

All of this Chakradar is contained in 2 full Tin Tal cycles of 16 Matras each, meaning 32 Matras or beats, plus 1 more beat at the beginning of the next Tala cycle – in which it ends –, with a total of 33 Matras.

Here is just one example of phrases:

CHAKRADAR TIHAI: *Chakra* significa en sánscrito 'rueda' o 'giro', Chakradar por lo tanto se traduciría 'giro sobre giro' o 'Tihai que gira'. Éste es el sentido del Chakradar Tihai, y marca el final definitivo de una obra.

Este ejemplo en particular de Chakradar Tihai consiste de 1 frase que se repite 3 veces con una pausa que dura 1/2 Matra entre las repeticiones; a su vez estas 3 frases en bloque se repiten 3 veces más.

Todo este Chakradar Tihai está insertado en 2 vueltas completas del ciclo rítmico Tin Tal de 16 tiempos, o sea 32 Matras; mas otro Matra al principio del siguiente Tala en el cual finaliza, lo que hace un total de 33 Matras.

Esta es una de las muchas frases que pueden utilizarse para el Chakradar:

D̲H̲A̲ T̲I̲N̲A̲ G̲A̲D̲H̲I̲ G̲I̲N̲A̲ | D̲H̲A̲ - G̲A̲D̲H̲I̲ G̲I̲N̲A̲ D̲H̲A̲ - | G̲A̲D̲H̲I̲ G̲I̲N̲A̲ D̲H̲A̲ -

EXAMPLE 33   **EJEMPLO 33**

TRACK **33** DISK **01**

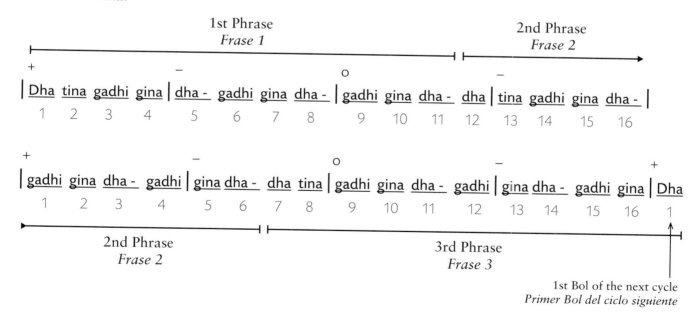

Note: Please have as a rule to use vocal recitation and finger counting with every Tihai form first, and then go ahead using the Tabla set.

Nota: Tratar de tomar como regla el recitar y solfear rítmicamente cada ejemplo de Tihai dado, y luego llevarlo al Tabla set y tocarlo.

THEKA

The word *Theka* means a fixed pattern of percussion that depicts the Matras or beats of a Tala – rhythmic cycle, and its divisions in Vibhags or bars and accents.

For example, the Theka corresponding to the Tin Tal graphically expresses for the listener of a performance all the subdivisions of the rhythmic cycle in 4 groups, bars or Vibhags; each of them has 4 Matras or beats. In the same way, it is possible to describe with Theka the rest of the Talas or rhythmic cycles.

Theka also establishes the Tempo of the performance, because it's always played at the beginning of any specific composition. The distinctions between resonant (full) and non-resonant (empty) Bols or strokes are clearly exposed by the presentation of the different Vibhags (bars) and Matras (beats) that belong to a Tala.

The following example shows the basic form of the *Tin Tal Theka* – 16 Matras.

As expressed before, the Theka is always performed as a presentation of the Tala, and before any composition. Theka establishes the 'Tempo' (for example, for a Kaida) and shows the characteristics of the Tala that is contained in the Theka.

THEKA

El término *Theka* significa un patrón fijo de percusión que indica los Matras o tiempos del ciclo rítmico y sus divisiones en Vibhags o compases.

El Theka para Tin Tal por ejemplo, delinea gráficamente para el que escucha las subdivisiones del ciclo rítmico en 4 grupos – Vibhags – de 4 matras cada uno. De la misma manera es posible describir en Theka a todos los demás Talas.

Un Theka también establece la velocidad de la interpretación previo a la presentación de una composición específica. La distinción entre resonantes y no resonantes se indica claramente también con el agrupamiento de los Matras – tiempos – en Vibhags o compases pertenecientes a un Tala.

En su forma básica el *Theka para Tin Tal* es descrito en el gráfico de la siguiente manera.

Como expresado anteriormente, el Theka se interpreta siempre antes de la presentación de un Tala previo a una composición (por ejemplo, un Kaida). Este establece el 'Tempo' para el Kaida y define las características del ciclo rítmico que está contenido en él.

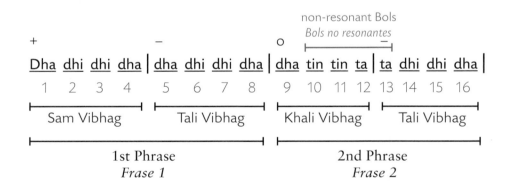

The following is an example from the Theme of the *Kaida 2* in Tin Tal, which is exposed later in the *Kaidas – Fixed Compositions* section, CHAPTER III. It has a direct connection with the last given example of Theka in Tin Tal:

El siguiente es un ejemplo tomado de un Tema del *Kaida 2* en Tin Tal, el cual se expone mas adelante en la sección *Kaidas – Composiciones Fijas* del CAPÍTULO III. Este tiene una conexión directa con el ejemplo anterior de Theka en Tin Tal:

EXAMPLE 34   **EJEMPLO 34**

TRACK
34
DISK
01

Tin Tal – 16 Matras

+				–				o				–			
Dha	dhi	dhi	dha	dha	dhi	dhi	dha	dha	tin	tin	ta	ta	dhi	dhi	dha
1	2	3	4	5	6	7	8	9	10	11	12	13	14	15	16

Kaida 2 – Theme | *Tema*

Khali Vibhag
non-resonant Bols
Bols no resonantes

+				–				o				–			
Dhana	gena	tina	gena	tina	tirikita	dhage	tuna	tata	kena	tina	kena	tina	tirikita	dhage	dhinna
1	2	3	4	5	6	7	8	9	10	11	12	13	14	15	16

|—— 1st Phrase / *Frase 1* ——|—— 2nd Phrase / *Frase 2* ——|

It is also possible that a musician decides on the spot to multiply or double the speed of the Kaida. If this happens, those 2 Kaida phrases will fit twice into just one Theka. This will resound to the listener as a sort of a 'compacted synthesis' from its original structure.

In fact, the Vibhags dimension is reduced, and the places for resonant / non-resonant Bols and accents are displaced in relation to the basic Tala structure.

The following is an example using the 2 Kaida phrases shown before.

O si el músico prefiere, el tempo del Kaida puede ser incrementado al doble. Si así ocurre, las 2 frases del Kaida entrarán 2 veces dentro del largo de un solo Theka. Para el que escucha esto resulta como una 'síntesis compacta' de su estructura original.

En efecto, las dimensiones de los Vibhags se reducen y los lugares de los Bols resonantes y no resonantes se desplazan con relación al Tala básico.

El siguiente es un ejemplo utilizando las 2 frases del Kaida expuesto anteriormente:

EXAMPLE 35   **EJEMPLO 35**

TRACK
35
DISK
01

Tin Tal Theka – 16 Matras

+				–				o				–			
Dha	dhi	dhi	dha	dha	dhi	dhi	dha	dha	tin	tin	ta	ta	dhi	dhi	dha
1	2	3	4	5	6	7	8	9	10	11	12	13	14	15	16

Kaida – Theme in **Drut Lay** or fast speed | *Tema en **Drut Lay** o velocidad rápida*

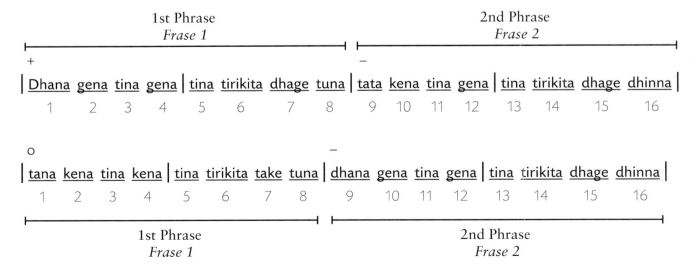

|—— 1st Phrase / *Frase 1* ——|—— 2nd Phrase / *Frase 2* ——|

+								–							
Dhana	gena	tina	gena	tina	tirikita	dhage	tuna	tata	kena	tina	gena	tina	tirikita	dhage	dhinna
1	2	3	4	5	6	7	8	9	10	11	12	13	14	15	16

o								–							
tana	kena	tina	kena	tina	tirikita	take	tuna	dhana	gena	tina	gena	tina	tirikita	dhage	dhinna
1	2	3	4	5	6	7	8	9	10	11	12	13	14	15	16

|—— 1st Phrase / *Frase 1* ——|—— 2nd Phrase / *Frase 2* ——|

TUNING THE TABLA

This section shows one of the most important lessons, regarding the care of the instrument, and a very important step toward its musical, artistic and aesthetic implications. It is always a difficult task to have a well tuned Tabla.

It is essential to achieve a certain degree of concentration and a good, sensitive hearing, in order to figure out how to adjust both Dayan and Bayan drums with a uniform tuning.

This is also indispensable when you play along with other musicians, singers or with instruments, for example *Sitar, Tampura, Harmonium, Sarod, Bansuri Flute, Violin, Sarangi, Shennai, Guitar, Piano,* etc. In the case of playing a Tabla Solo, it is always good to have the aid of a tuner.

Thus, the Dayan should always be tuned in relation to the main note or chord of a *Raga* or composition. This principal note is called a *Shadaja* or **Sa**, from the *Sa Re Ga Ma Pa Da Ni* of Indian music notation. For example in a Tabla Solo, when accompanied by a Tampura drone – a 4 or 5 stringed instrument without frets tuned in one fixed chord, like C sharp (C♯) or D with its 4th or 5th harmonic notes. This *Sa* is usually recognized as a background drone or *pedal* sound, in almost every Industani music performance.

The Sa could also be tuned in A, B, B♭, C, E, F, or G, always depending on which chord the other instruments or singers are going to perform. The basic root-note Sa in Indian music is the main tune with which musicians based their musical performances.

This form of fixed harmony in one chord is called in western terminology '*Modal Form*', and is the fundamental chord that musicians use as a basic platform for their interpretations.

The high pitch **Dayan** is usually tuned with the Bol **Ta** or **Tin**, because of its open sound that has the harmonics needed to tune this drum.

The range in which the Dayan can be tuned depends on its size; Dayan with smaller heads are higher in their pitch than bigger Dayan. The diameter of a Dayan circumference ranges between 4, and 6 1/2 inches.

In the past, musicians used to play with bigger Dayan more often, but in our days smaller ones are preferred because of its lighter sound for a more modern instrumental accompaniment, about 5 or 5 1/4 inches. These Dayan have a brighter and higher pitch sound, compared to the bigger ones, but for Tabla Solo concerts, it's still the bigger Dayan that many choose to play, for its noble and characteristic lower and profound sound.

AFINACIÓN DEL TABLA

Esta sección es una de las más importantes lecciones a tener en cuenta en lo que respecta al cuidado del instrumento, y un paso muy importante en el aspecto musical, artístico y estético. Es siempre un asunto difícil el lograr tener un Tabla bien afinado.

Es por lo tanto esencial un cierto grado de desarrollo auditivo y de concentración – o lo que se llama 'un buen oído' –, para lograr encontrar la forma de ajustar ambos tambores – Dayan y Bayan – con un sonido afinado y uniforme.

Esto también es indispensable cuando se esta tocando con otros músicos, cantantes o con instrumentos, como por ejemplo: *Sitar, Tampura, Armonio, Sarod, Flauta Bansuri, Violín, Sarangi, Shennai, Guitarra, Piano,* etc. En el caso de tocar un solo de Tabla, siempre es bueno contar con un afinador.

Por lo tanto, la afinación del Dayan debe de estar siempre conforme al tono o acorde principal de un *Raga* o composición. Este tono principal se denomina *Shadaja* o **Sa** de la notación melódica *Sa Ri Ga Ma Pa Da Ni* en la música India. Por ejemplo en un solo de Tabla, cuando se le acompaña con un pedal Tampura – un instrumento de 4 o 5 cuerdas sin trastes, y afinado en base a una sola nota o acorde, como Do sostenido (C♯) o Re, con sus respectivas 4tas y 5tas notas. Este *Sa* es generalmente reconocido como el sonido *pedal* (bajo continuo) o de fondo, en casi toda interpretación de la música Indostánica.

El Sa puede ser también A, B, B♭, C, E, F, o G, etc. y así adaptarse a las tonalidades que cada instrumentista o cantante elija para tocar. El Sa en la música de la India es principalmente la nota base en la que los músicos basan su interpretación.

Esta forma de armonía fija o interpretación en un solo acorde fijo se denomina en occidente como '*Forma Modal*' y es el acorde fundamental que los músicos utilizan como plataforma básica en sus interpretaciones.

Para afinar el **Dayan** se utilizan básicamente los Bols **Ta** y **Tin**, ya que gracias al sonido abierto que poseen, producen los armónicos del tono fundamental al que éste debe ser afinado.

El rango de afinación al que el Dayan se puede acomodar dependiendo del tamaño del parche. Dayan mas pequeños dan notas mas agudas que los mas anchos. El diámetro de la circunferencia de un Dayan oscila entre 4, y 6 1/2 pulgadas, unos 10 y 18 centímetros respectivamente.

En el pasado, los músicos preferían tocar Dayan mas grandes, pero los Dayan de tamaño más pequeño son los más populares hoy en día, debido a su sonido más liviano y moderno para acompañamiento instrumental, con un diámetro de aproximadamente 5 o 5 1/4 pulgadas – 12 a 15 centímetros. Estos producen sonidos más brillantes y agudos en comparación con los de diámetro más

The following are tuning ranges for Dayan that has between 5 to 6 1/2 inches diameter:

5 inches: middle C to F
5 1/4 inches: B to D♯
5 1/2 inches: A to D
6 to 6 1/2 inches: G to C

Note: These tuning ranges are estimates based on the author's experience.

grande, aunque estos últimos se siguen utilizando en algunos conciertos de Tabla Solo, por su característico sonido más noble y profundo.

Los siguientes son rangos de afinación para tambores Dayan de entre 5 y 6 1/2 pulgadas / 12 a 18 centímetros:

12 cm: Do central a Fa (5 pulgadas: C a F)
14 cm: Si a Re sostenido (5 1/4 pulgadas: B a D♯)
16 cm: La a Re (5 1/2 pulgadas: A a D)
18 cm: Sol a Do (6 a 6 1/2 pulgadas: G a C)

Nota: estas estimaciones están basadas en la experiencia personal del autor de éste método.

EXAMPLE 36: DAYAN

EJEMPLO 36: DAYAN

TRACK
36
DISK
01

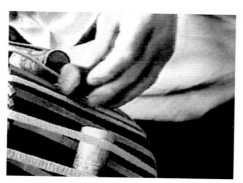

1

Adjust the **Ghattas** or wooden cylinders.

*Ajustar los **Ghattas** o cilindros de madera*

2

First, tune the Ghattas with the hammer by striking down to raise, or up to lower the pitch of the Dayan.

Afinar los Ghattas martillando hacia abajo para subir, o hacia arriba para bajar el tono del Dayan.

3

Strike the lower part of the head's external ring – or **Pagri** – upwards, to lower the pitch of the Dayan.

*Martillar hacia arriba el costado inferior del anillo exterior del parche – o **Pagri** – para bajar el tono del Dayan.*

4

Strike the upper side of the Pagri downwards to raise the pitch of the Dayan.

Martillar hacia abajo la cara superior del Pagri para subir el tono del Dayan.

A small *hammer* is used for tuning the drums, hitting the *Gattha* or small cylinders that are placed in between the leather strings. When one hits the Gattha downward the pitch of the Dayan's head goes higher; and when hitting upward, the pitch goes lower and the tension is released from the head.

A more subtle way for tuning is by hitting with the hammer the external ring that goes around the drumhead, called *Pagri*. This stage of tuning requires a good amount of patience and focus from the student.

A good suggestion is to practice tuning, especially the Dayan, for as long as you can, paying attention and adjusting the sound as it comes, in order to increase the accuracy of the performances. An out-of-tune Tabla often makes the audience feel 'uncomfortable', and a good tuned Tabla is always a sign of a good musician.

It's again recommended to have a melodic or harmonic instrument at hand that can give the correct tune (or a tuner) if you're not with other musicians.

Finally, some words on the low pitch **Bayan** tuning: This drum is much easier to tune than a Dayan because it comes with a natural tune, which is around the lower F, G or A notes (below middle C), depending on the different sizes, shapes and qualities. It's still possible to tune the Bayan by slightly hammering around the Pagri or drumhead external ring, in the same way as with the Dayan.

Usually both Dayan and Bayan drums are tuned at an interval of a 4th or 5th note, for example: Dayan tuned in middle C, Bayan in G or F below middle C, etc.

Para afinar los tambores se utiliza un *martillo* pequeño, para golpear los *Gatthas* o cilindros de madera que se encuentran trenzados entre la cuerda de cuero. Se martilla el Gattha hacia abajo para subir el tono del Dayan, y hacia arriba para bajar el tono y aflojar así la tensión del parche.

El ajuste más fino se logra dando golpes suaves con el martillo alrededor del anillo exterior que bordea el parche, denominado *Pagri*. Esta etapa de la afinación requiere de mucha paciencia y atención por parte del músico estudiante.

Una buena sugerencia es practicar la afinación, especialmente del Dayan, el mayor tiempo posible, prestando atención al sonido y ajustándolo, buscando incrementar la eficacia de lo interpretado. Un Tabla 'desafinado' suele hacer sentir incomoda a la audiencia, mientras que un Tabla bien afinado es siempre el signo de un buen músico.

Se recomienda nuevamente tener a mano un instrumento armónico o melódico que dé la nota exacta (o un afinador) si es que no hay otro músico que la pueda dar.

Finalmente unas palabras acerca de la afinación del tambor grave o **Bayan**. Éste es más fácil de ajustar que el Dayan porque posee una afinación natural, la cual se ubica entre las notas Fa, Sol y La de la octava anterior al Do central, dependiendo de los distintos tamaños, formas y calidades. De todas maneras, es posible afinar el Bayan dando suaves golpes con el martillo alrededor del Pagri o anillo externo que bordea el parche, de la misma forma que con el Dayan.

Usualmente los dos Dayan y Bayan se afinan un intervalo de 4ta o 5ta, por ejemplo: Dayan en Do central, Bayan en Sol o Fa de la octava anterior al Do central, etc.

BAYAN

BAYAN

5 & 6: To tune the Bayan, slightly hammer around the Pagri or drumhead external ring,

Para afinar el Bayan, dar golpes suaves con el martillo alrededor del Pagri o anillo externo del parche.

7 & 8: If you have a **cotton chord** that holds the leather head to the body of the Bayan, use the set of metal rings that come interlaced with the chord to increase or decrease the tension. Or, if you have a **leather chord**, try to insert some small wooden blocks between the leather chord and the body of the Bayan, in order to adjust the tune in a similar way as with the Dayan.

*Si el Bayan tiene como sujetador del parche una **cuerda de algodón**, utilizar los anillos de metal que vienen entrelazados para aumentar o aflojar la tensión en el parche. Si el Bayan tiene en cambio **tientos de cuero**, tratar de insertar unos pequeños cilindros de madera entre el tiento y el cuerpo del tambor para ajustar la entonación, como en el Dayan.*

TALAS – PRACTICE SECTION

The following is a list with some of the most popular rhythmic cycles or *Talas* used in the Industani music system. They are depicted with Bols and beat numbers (Matras), also including at the bottom pictures of the '*Keeping Tala*' hand gestures, for a better understanding of the solfege on each Tala.

We start with the *16 beats Tin Tal*, maybe the most popular and relevant of the Talas, that has already been analyzed extensively throughout this method.

TALAS – PARTE PRÁCTICA

Continuamos con una lista que incluye algunos de los Talas más populares dentro del sistema musical Indostánico. Pueden verse descritos con sus Bols y números de tiempo (Matras); también incluyen fotos de los gestos de las manos para el '*Solfeo de Tala*', para una mejor comprensión de esta técnica de solfeo.

Comenzamos con el *Tin Tal de 16 Matras*, quizá el más importante y popular de los Talas, y que hemos desarrollado extensivamente a lo largo de este método.

EXAMPLE 37

EJEMPLO 37

Track 37 · Disk 01

Tin Tal – 16 Matras, 4 Vibhags

+				–				o				–			
Dha	dhi	dhi	dha	dha	dhi	dhi	dha	dha	tin	tin	ta	ta	dhi	dhi	dha
1	2	3	4	5	6	7	8	9	10	11	12	13	14	15	16

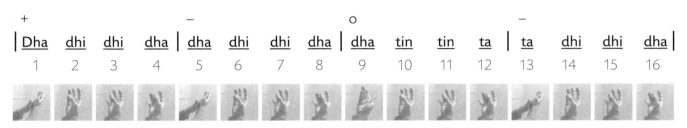

EXAMPLE 38

EJEMPLO 38

Track 38 · Disk 01

Dadra Tal – 6 Matras, 2 Vibhags

+		o	–		
Dha	dhi	na	dha	ti	na
1	2	3	4	5	6

EXAMPLE 39

EJEMPLO 39

Track 39 · Disk 01

Roopak Tal | *Rupak Tal* – 7 Matras, 3 Vibhags

This Tal has no *Sam*, or it's merged with the *Khali*.
It is one of the exceptions within the Industani Tala system.

Este Tal no tiene Sam, *o mejor dicho, está fusionado con el* Khali.
Es una de las excepciones dentro del sistema de Talas Indostánico.

o (+)			–		–	
Tin	tin	na	dhi	na	dhi	na
1	2	3	4	5	6	7

EXAMPLE 40   EJEMPLO 40

TRACK
40
DISK
01

Kherwa Tal – 8 Matras, 2 Vibhags

+		−		o		−	
Dha	ge	na	ti	ta	ke	dhin	na
1	2	3	4	5	6	7	8

EXAMPLE 41   EJEMPLO 41

TRACK
41
DISK
01

Latin Tal – 8 Matras, 2 Vibhags.   Composed by | *Compuesto por*: R. Hambra ©1997

+		−		o		−	
Dha -	nage	tita	ketin	- ta	kena	nage	dhina
1	2	3	4	5	6	7	8

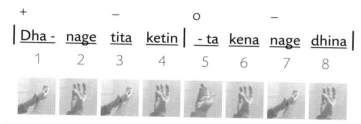

EXAMPLE 42   EJEMPLO 42

TRACK
42
DISK
01

Jhup Tal – 10 Matras, 4 Vibhags

+			−		o		−		
Dhi	na	dhi	dhi	na	tin	na	dhi	dhi	na
1	2	3	4	5	6	7	8	9	10

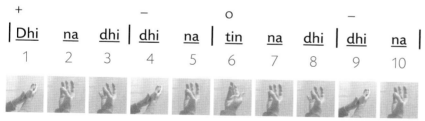

EXAMPLE 43   EJEMPLO 43

TRACK
43
DISK
01

Sulfakhta Tal – 10 Matras, 5 Vibhags

+		o		−		−		−	
Dha	dha	dhi	ta	kita	dha	tite	kata	gadi	gena
1	2	3	4	5	6	7	8	9	10

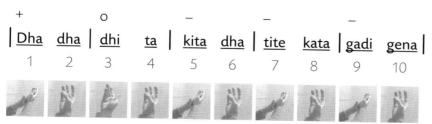

EXAMPLE 44   EJEMPLO 44

TRACK
44
DISK
01

Char Tal Ki Sawari – 11 Matras, 11 Vibhags

+		–		–		o		–		–	

Dhi - - kri	dhita	dhidhi	na - trikri	dhita	dhidhi	na - dhage	nadhagena	dhi - ta	- dhi	- ta
1	2	3	4	5	6	7	8	9	10	11

EXAMPLE 45   EJEMPLO 45

TRACK
45
DISK
01

Ek Tal – 12 Matras, 4 Vibhags

+				o				–		–	

Dhi	dhi	dhage	tirikita	tun	na	ka	ta	dhage	tirikita	dhi	na
1	2	3	4	5	6	7	8	9	10	11	12

EXAMPLE 46   EJEMPLO 46

TRACK
46
DISK
01

Char Tal – 12 Matras, 6 Vibhags

+		o		–		o		–		–	

Dha	dha	dhi	ta	kita	dha	dhi	ta	tite	kata	gadi	gena
1	2	3	4	5	6	7	8	9	10	11	12

EXAMPLE 47   EJEMPLO 47

TRACK
47
DISK
01

Deepchandi Tal – 14 Matras, 4 Vibhags

+			–			o			–				

Dha	dhi	-	dha	ge	ti	-	ta	tin	-	dha	ge	dhi	-
1	2	3	4	5	6	7	8	9	10	11	12	13	14

EXAMPLE 48   EJEMPLO 48

TRACK
01
DISK
02

Jhumra Tal – 14 Matras, 4 Vibhags

+			–				o			–			
Dhi	dhi	dhage	dhi	dhi	dhage	tirikita	tin	tin	take	dhi	dhi	dhage	tirikita
1	2	3	4	5	6	7	8	9	10	11	12	13	14

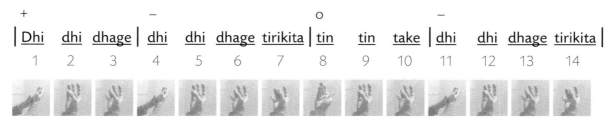

EXAMPLE 49   EJEMPLO 49

TRACK
02
DISK
02

Dhamar Tal – 14 Matras, 4 Vibhags

+					–		o			–			
Ka	dhi	ta	dhi	ta	dha	-	ge	dhin	na	dhi	na	ta	-
1	2	3	4	5	6	7	8	9	10	11	12	13	14

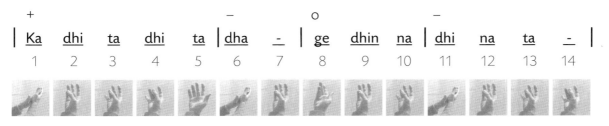

EXAMPLE 50   EJEMPLO 50

TRACK
03
DISK
02

Ada Chautal – 14 Matras, 7 Vibhags

+		–		o		–		–			–	–	
Dhi	trik	dhi	na	tu	na	ka	ta	trik	dhi	na	dhi	dhi	na
1	2	3	4	5	6	7	8	9	10	11	12	13	14

Note: The Bol TRIK *is explained in detail in the 'More Bols for Advanced Practice' section in this method.*

Nota: El Bol TRIK *se expone en detalle en la sección 'Más Bols para Práctica Avanzada' en este método.*

EXAMPLE 51   EJEMPLO 51

TRACK
04
DISK
02

Bulería Tal – 12 Matras, 5 Vibhags.   Composed by | *Compuesto por*: R. Hambra ©2000

o (+)			–			–	–		–		–	
Ti	te	dha	ti	te	ti	dha	dha	ti	dha	ti	dha
1	2	3	4	5	6	7	8	9	10	1(11)	2(12)

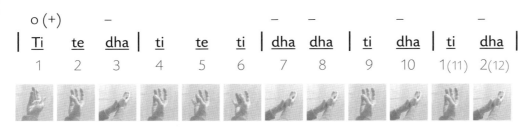

EXAMPLE 52   **EJEMPLO 52**

TRACK
05
DISK
02

Tango Tal – 8 Matras, 4 Vibhags.   Composed by | *Compuesto por*: R. Hambra ©2006

+		o		—		—	
Dha	ti	te	tirikita	dhita	dhidhi	ta	-
1	2	3	4	5	6	7	8

EXAMPLE 53   **EJEMPLO 53**

TRACK
06
DISK
02

Samba Tal – 8 Matras, 2 Vibhags.   Composed by | *Compuesto por*: R. Hambra ©2006

o		—		—			
Kat	- ta	ge	ta	ka	ta	dhita	-
1	2	3	4	5	6	7	8

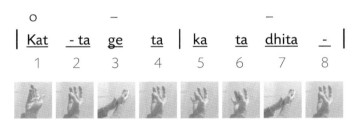

KAIDAS – FIXED COMPOSITIONS
- composed by Ricardo Hambra © 2011 -

The time has come to start working directly with the *Fixed Compositions* called *Kaidas*.

The following is a series of different Kaidas based on different *Talas*, and each one with their own development sections: *Theka, Tala, Theme, Variations* and *Tihai*.

Notice that in order to be able to understand these compositions, it is essential to learn first all the previous sections of this method. That means first to develop the skills to manage good sounding *Bols* or strokes, then all the exercises, and afterwards some of the Talas shown earlier, in CHAPTER II, practice section of this method.

Anyhow, it is recommended to first read and recite the Kaidas out loud, along with the CD examples, even if you don't have yet the skills to perform them. The accentuation of all the Themes, Variations and Tihai of each Kaida, is established by their respective Theka Tal. Pay attention to the audio examples, where it is possible to listen to the Theka Tal counting on every Tala and Kaida depicted in *Tabla for All*. By its recitation and rhythmic solfege, you may be able to have a first approach to the beautiful rhythmic poetry that is a characteristic of this kind of musical compositions. Good Luck!

Note: In all of the following Kaidas, keep counting the Tal Theka throughout the entire composition.

KAIDAS – COMPOSICIONES FIJAS
- compuestos por Ricardo Hambra © 2011 -

Llegó el momento de comenzar a trabajar directamente con las *Composiciones Fijas* llamadas *Kaidas*.

Los siguientes son una serie de distintos Kaidas basados en diferentes *Talas*, cada uno con su desarrollo: *Theka, Tal, Tema principal, Variaciones* y *Tihai*.

Notar que para poder comprender su interpretación es indispensable una etapa previa de preparación y estudio de los *Bols* y ejemplos explicados previamente en este método. Esto significa que primero se debe desarrollar la tecnica y la habilidad para tocar bien los Bols, luego practicar los ejercicios, así como algunos de los diferentes Talas ya analizados en el CAPÍTULO II, parte práctica de este método.

De todas maneras, se recomienda leer y recitar los Kaidas en voz alta, acompañandose con los ejemplos de los CDs, incluso si aún no se posee la destreza para poderlos tocar. La acentuación de todos los Temas, Variaciones y Tihai de cada Kaida, es establecida por su respectivo Theka Tal. Prestar atención a los ejemplos de audio, donde se puede escuchar el conteo de Theka Tal en todos los Talas y Kaidas descritos en *Tabla para Todos*. Mediante el recitado y el solfeo ritmico se podrá tener una primera idea de la bella poesía rítmica característica en este tipo de composiciones. ¡Buena Suerte!

Nota: En todos los Kaidas que siguen, continuar con el conteo del Tal Theka durante toda la composición.

TRACK **07** DISK **02**

Tin tal

16 Matras, 4 Vibhags

Ricardo Hambra

EXAMPLE 54 – KAIDA 1

- Tin Tal Theka: 4 times,
- Kaida Theme: 4 times,
- Tin Tal Theka: 1 time,
- Variations: 2 times each proceeded by Tin Tal theka 1 time after each variation.
- Tihai

EJEMPLO 54 – KAIDA 1

- Tin Tal Theka: 4 ciclos,
- Kaida Tema: 4 ciclos,
- Tin Tal Theka: 1 ciclo,
- Variaciones: 2 ciclos cada una, seguido por 1 ciclo de Tin Tal theka luego de cada variación.
- Tihai

Tin Tal – 16 Matras

```
      +                    –                    o                    –
    | Dha  dhi  dhi  dha | dha  dhi  dhi  dha | dha  tin  tin  ta | ta  dhi  dhi  dha |
       1    2    3    4     5    6    7    8     9   10   11   12   13  14   15   16
```

Metronome: ♩ = 70

Kaida 1: Theme | *Tema*

```
      +                      –                      o                      –
    | Dhage  tite  dhina  gina | dhage  na -  tina  kata | take  tite  tina  kina | dhage  na -  dhina  gena |
        1      2     3     4       5     6    7     8        9    10    11    12      13    14    15    16
```

Variations | *Variaciones*

```
        +                           3                       o                    2
1   ( Dhage  tite  dhina  gina ) | dhage  na -  tina  kata | ( take  tite  tina  kina ) | dhage  tite  dhina  gina |

    dhage  na -  dhina  gena | }
```

```
        +
2   Dhage  tite  dhina  gina | dhati  dha -  dhati  dha - | dhage  tite  dhina  gina | dhage  na -  tina  kata |

    o
    take  tite  tina  kina | tati  ta -  tati  ta - | dhage  tite  dhina  gina | dhage  na -  dhina  gena | }
```

3

+

<u>Dhadha</u> <u>- dha</u> <u>tite</u> <u>tite</u> | <u>dha -</u> <u>- dha</u> <u>tite</u> <u>tite</u> | <u>dhadha</u> <u>- dha</u> <u>tite</u> <u>tite</u> | <u>dhage</u> <u>na -</u> <u>tina</u> <u>kata</u> |

o

<u>tata</u> <u>- ta</u> <u>tite</u> <u>tite</u> | <u>ta -</u> <u>- ta</u> <u>tite</u> <u>tite</u> | <u>dhadha</u> <u>- dha</u> <u>tite</u> <u>tite</u> | <u>dhage</u> <u>na -</u> <u>dhina</u> <u>gena</u> | }

4

+   3   2

<u>Dhage</u> (<u>tite</u>) <u>dhage</u> (<u>tite</u>) <u>dhage</u> | <u>tite</u> <u>dhati</u> <u>dha -</u> <u>dha -</u> | <u>dhage</u> <u>na -</u> <u>tina</u> <u>kata</u> |

o   3   2

<u>take</u> (<u>tite</u>) <u>take</u> (<u>tite</u>) <u>take</u> | <u>tite</u> <u>dhati</u> <u>dha -</u> <u>dha -</u> | <u>dhage</u> <u>na -</u> <u>dhina</u> <u>gena</u> | }

5

+   3

(<u>Dhage</u> <u>tite</u>) <u>dhadha</u> <u>tina</u> | <u>dha - tiri</u> <u>kitetake</u> <u>tirikita</u> <u>dha -</u> | <u>dhage</u> <u>na -</u> <u>tina</u> <u>kata</u> |

o   3

(<u>take</u> <u>tite</u>) <u>tata</u> <u>tina</u> | <u>dha - tiri</u> <u>kitetake</u> <u>tirikita</u> <u>dha -</u> | <u>dhage</u> <u>na -</u> <u>dhina</u> <u>gena</u> | }

Tihai

+   (+)   3x

[<u>Dhage</u> <u>tite</u> <u>dhadha</u> <u>- ti</u> <u>- na</u> | <u>dhage</u> <u>tite</u> <u>dhadha</u> <u>- ti</u> <u>- na</u> <u>dha</u>]

Tin tal
16 Matras, 4 Vibhags

Ricardo Hambra

EXAMPLE 55 – KAIDA 2

• Tin Tal Theka: 4 times,
• Kaida Theme: 4 times,
• Tin Tal Theka: 1 time,
• Variations: 2 times each proceeded by Tin Tal Theka 1 time after each variation.
• Tihai

EJEMPLO 55 – KAIDA 2

• Tin Tal Theka: 4 ciclos,
• Kaida Tema: 4 ciclos,
• Tin Tal Theka: 1 ciclo,
• Variaciones: 2 ciclos cada una, seguido por 1 ciclo de Tin Tal theka luego de cada variación.
• Tihai

Tin Tal – 16 Matras

+				–				o				–			
Dha	dhi	dhi	dha	dha	dhi	dhi	dha	dha	tin	tin	ta	ta	dhi	dhi	dha
1	2	3	4	5	6	7	8	9	10	11	12	13	14	15	16

Metronome: ♩ = 70

Kaida 2: Theme | *Tema*

+				–				o				–			
Dhana	gena	tina	gena	tina	tirikita	dhage	tuna	tana	kena	tina	gena	tina	tirikita	dhage	dhinna
1	2	3	4	5	6	7	8	9	10	11	12	13	14	15	16

Variations | *Variaciones*

1
+
Dhana gena tina dhana | gena tina dhana gena | tina gena tina gena | tina tirikita dhage tuna |

o
tana kena tina tana | kena tina tana kena | tina gena tina gena | tina tirikita dhage dhinna | }

2
+
Dhana gena dha - _ | dha - tiri kitetake tirikita dha - | dhana gena tina gena | tina tirikita dhage tuna |

o
tana kena ta - _ | ta - tiri kitetake tirikita ta - | dhana gena tina gena | tina tirikita dhage dhinna | }

3　⁺　　　　　　　2
(<u>Gena</u> <u>gena</u> <u>tina</u> <u>tirikita</u>) | <u>dhadha</u> <u>dha -</u> <u>tirikita</u> <u>taketa -</u> | <u>tina</u> <u>tirikita</u> <u>dhage</u> <u>tuna</u> |

　　o　　　　　　　2
(<u>kena</u> <u>kena</u> <u>tina</u> <u>tirikita</u>) | <u>dhadha</u> <u>dha -</u> <u>tirikita</u> <u>taketa -</u> | <u>tina</u> <u>tirikita</u> <u>dhage</u> <u>dhinna</u> | }

4　⁺
<u>Dhana</u> <u>dhana</u> <u>tina</u> <u>tirikita</u> | <u>dha - tiri</u> <u>kitetake</u> <u>tirikita</u> <u>dha - ti -</u> |

<u>dha - tiri</u> <u>kitetake</u> <u>tirikita</u> <u>dha - ti -</u> | <u>dha -</u> <u>tirikita</u> <u>dhage</u> <u>tuna</u> |

　　o
<u>nana</u> <u>nana</u> <u>tina</u> <u>tirikita</u> | <u>ta - tiri</u> <u>kitetake</u> <u>tirikita</u> <u>ta - ti -</u> |

<u>dha - tiri</u> <u>kitetake</u> <u>tirikita</u> <u>dha - ti -</u> | <u>dha -</u> <u>tirikita</u> <u>dhage</u> <u>dhinna</u> | }

Tihai

⁺　　　　　　　　　　　　　　　　　　　　　　　　(+)　3x
[<u>Dhana</u> <u>gena</u> <u>tina</u> <u>gena</u> <u>dha - tiri</u> | <u>kitetake</u> <u>tirikita</u> <u>dha - ti -</u> <u>dha - tiri</u> <u>kitadha -</u> <u>dha -</u>]

TRACK
09
DISK
02

Dadra Tal
6 Matras, 2 Vibhags

Ricardo Hambra

EXAMPLE 56 – KAIDA 3

- Dadra Tal Theka: 4 times,
- Kaida Theme: 4 times,
- Dadra Tal Theka: 1 time,
- Variations: 2 times each proceeded by Dadra Tal Theka 2 times after each variation.
- Tihai

EJEMPLO 56 – KAIDA 3

- Dadra Tal Theka: 4 ciclos,
- Kaida Tema: 4 ciclos,
- Dadra Tal Theka: 1 ciclo,
- Variaciones: 2 ciclos cada una, seguido por 2 ciclos de Dadra Tal theka luego de cada variación.
- Tihai

Dadra Tal – 6 Matras

```
    +           o     −
| Dha  dhi  na | dha  tin  na |
    1    2    3    4    5    6
```

Metronome: ♩ = 100

Kaida 3: Theme | *Tema*

```
    +                     −                         o                    −
| Dhati  tedha  tina | dha - tiri  kitadha  - tuna | tati  tete  tina | dha - tiri  kitadha  - dhina |
     1      2      3       4          5        6       7      8     9       10          11       12
```

Variations | *Variaciones*

```
     +              3
1  ( Dhati  tedha  tina ) | dha - tiri  kitadha  - tuna |

     o              2
   ( tati  tete  tina ) | dhati  tedha  tina | dha - tiri  kitadha  - dhina | }
```

```
     +              2
2  ( Dhati  tedha  tina ) | dha - tiri  kitadha -  tirikita | dha - tiri  kitadha -  _ | dha - tiri  kitadha  - tuna |

     o              2
   ( tati  teta  tina ) | dha - tiri  kitadha -  tirikita | dha - tiri  kitadha -  _ | dha - tiri  kitadha  - dhina | }
```

3 +
(<u>Dhati</u> <u>tedha</u> <u>tirikita</u>) | <u>dhati</u> <u>tedha</u> <u>- tuna</u> |
³

o
(<u>tati</u> <u>tete</u> <u>tirikita</u>) | <u>dhati</u> <u>tedha</u> <u>tirikita</u> | <u>dhati</u> <u>tedha</u> <u>- dhina</u> | }
²

4 +
(<u>Dhati</u> <u>tedha</u> <u>-</u> | <u>dha - tiri</u> <u>kitetake</u> <u>tirikita</u>) |
²

<u>taketiri</u> <u>kitetake</u> <u>tirikita</u> | <u>dha - tiri</u> <u>kitadha</u> <u>- tuna</u> |

o
<u>tati</u> <u>tita</u> <u>-</u> | <u>ta - tiri</u> <u>kitetake</u> <u>tirikita</u> | <u>dhati</u> <u>tedha</u> <u>-</u> | <u>dha - tiri</u> <u>kitetake</u> <u>tirikita</u> |

<u>taketiri</u> <u>kitetake</u> <u>tirikita</u> | <u>dha - tiri</u> <u>kitadha</u> <u>- dhina</u> | }

5 +
<u>Dhadha</u> <u>dhadha</u> <u>dhadha</u> | <u>dhati</u> <u>tedha</u> <u>-</u> | <u>dha - tiri</u> <u>kitetake</u> <u>tirikita</u> | <u>dha - tiri</u> <u>kitadha</u> <u>- tuna</u> |

o
<u>tata</u> <u>tata</u> <u>tata</u> | <u>tati</u> <u>tedha</u> <u>-</u> | <u>dha - tiri</u> <u>kitetake</u> <u>tirikita</u> | <u>dha - tiri</u> <u>kitadha</u> <u>- dhina</u> | }

Tihai

+
[<u>Dhati</u> <u>tedha</u> <u>tina</u> | (<u>dha - tiri</u> <u>kitetake</u> <u>tirikita</u>) |] <u>Dha</u>
³ 3x (+)

Roopak Tal
7 Matras, 3 Vibhags

Ricardo Hambra

EXAMPLE 57 – KAIDA 4

- Roopak Tal Theka: 4 times,
- Kaida Theme: 4 times,
- Roopak Tal Theka: 2 times,
- Variations: 2 times each proceeded by Roopak Tal Theka 2 times after each variation.
- Tihai

EJEMPLO 57 – KAIDA 4

- Roopak Tal Theka: 4 ciclos,
- Kaida Tema: 4 ciclos,
- Roopak Tal Theka: 2 cicloa,
- Variaciones: 2 ciclos cada una, seguido por 2 ciclos de Roopak Tal theka luego de cada variación.
- Tihai

Roopak Tal – 7 Matras

```
    o              –              –
| Tin  tin  na | dhi  na | dhi  na |
   1   2   3    4    5    6    7
```

Metronome: ♩ = 100

Kaida 4: Theme | *Tema*

```
(+) o                        –              –
| Dhi - na  dhi - na  dhatirikita | dhi - na  dhageti | rikita  dha - |
    1         2          3           4        5          6      7
```

Variations | *Variaciones*

```
   (+) o                        3                    2
1  ( Dhi - na  dhi - na  dhatirikita ) | dhi - na | ( dhageti  rikita ) | }
```

```
   (+) o                   2                2
2  ( Dhi - na | dhatirikita ) ( dhageti  rikita ) | dhi - na  dhatirikita | dhageti  rikita | kataga  dhigena | }
```

3
$$\overset{(+)\ o}{(\ \underline{Dhi\text{-}dhi}}\ |\ \overset{2}{\underline{\text{-}na}}\ )\ (\ \underline{dhadha}\ |\ \overset{2}{\underline{tirikita}}\ )\ |\ \underline{dhi\text{-}na}\ \underline{dhatirikita}\ |\ \underline{dhageti}\ \underline{rikita}\ |\ \underline{kataga}\ \underline{dhigena}\ |\ \}$$

4
$$\overset{(+)\ o}{\underline{Dhi\text{-}na}}\ \underline{dhi\text{-}na}\ \underline{dhatirikita}\ |\ \underline{dhi\text{-}na}\ (\ \underline{dhatirikita}\ |\ \underline{taketirikita}\ \overset{2}{\underline{dha\text{-}}}\ )\ |$$

$$\underline{dhatirikita}\ |\ \underline{taketirikita}\ |\ \underline{kataga}\ \underline{dhigena}\ |\ \}$$

Tihai

$$\overset{(+)\ o}{\underline{Dhi\text{-}na}}\ \underline{dhi\text{-}na}\ \underline{dhatirikita}\ |\ \underline{taketirikita}\ \underline{dha\text{-}na}\ |\ \underline{dhi\text{-}na}\ \underline{dhi\text{-}na}\ |\ \overset{o}{\underline{dhatirikita}}\ \underline{taketirikita}\ \underline{dha\text{-}na}\ |$$

$$\underline{dhi\text{-}na}\ \underline{dhi\text{-}na}\ |\ \underline{dhatirikita}\ \underline{taketirikita}\ |\ \overset{(+)}{\underline{Tin}}$$

Kherwa Tal
8 Matras, 2 Vibhags

Ricardo Hambra

EXAMPLE 58 – KAIDA 5	**EJEMPLO 58 – KAIDA 5**

• Kherwa Tal Theka: 4 times,
• Kaida Theme: 4 times,
• Kherwa Tal Theka: 4 times,
• Variations: 2 times each proceeded by Kherwa Tal Theka 4 times after each variation.
• Tihai

• Kherwa Tal Theka: 4 ciclos,
• Kaida Tema: 4 ciclos,
• Kherwa Tal Theka: 4 ciclos,
• Variaciones: 2 ciclos cada una, seguido por 4 ciclos de Kherwa Tal theka luego de cada variación.
• Tihai

Kherwa Tal – 8 Matras

```
     +         –       o      –
 | Dha ge na ti | ta ke dhin na |
   1  2  3  4   5  6   7   8
```

Metronome: ♩ = 100

Kaida 5: Theme | *Tema*

```
   +                         –                          o                          –
 | Dha - tiri kita dha - | dhin - nana keke tite | ta - tiri kita dha - | dhin - nana gege tite |
    1    2    3    4        5     6    7    8       9   10   11   12        13     14   15   16
```

Variations | *Variaciones*

```
        +                        3
 1  ( Dha - tiri kita dha - ) | dhin - nana keke tite |

    o                        2
   ( ta - tiri kita ta - ) | dha - tiri kita dha - | dhin - nana gege tite | }
```

```
        +
 2  Dha - tiri kita dhadha | - tiri kita dhadha | dha - tiri kita dha - | dhin - nana keke tite |

    o
   ta - tiri kita tata | - tiri kita tata | dha - tiri kita dha - | dhin - nana gege tite | }
```

+

3 Dha - tiri kita dha - | tite tite tite dha - | dha - tiri kita dha - | dhin - nana keke tite |

o

ta - tiri kita ta - | tite tite tite ta - | dha - tiri kita dha - | dhin - nana gege tite | }

+

4 Dha - tiri kita dha - | tite tite tite dha - | tite tite dha - - | dhin - nana keke tite |

o

ta - tiri kita ta - | tite tite tite ta - | tite tite dha - - | dhin - nana gege tite | }

Tihai

+

Dha - tiri kita tite | tite dha - tiri kita | tite tite dha - tiri | kita tite tite tite | Dha ⁽⁺⁾

Jhup Tal
10 Matras, 4 Vibhags

Ricardo Hambra

EXAMPLE 59 – KAIDA 6

- Jhup Tal Theka: 4 times,
- Kaida Theme: 4 times,
- Jhup Tal Theka: 2 times,
- Variations: 2 times each proceeded by Jhup Tal Theka 2 times after each variation.
- Tihai

EJEMPLO 59 – KAIDA 6

- Jhup (pronunciar 'Yap') Tal Theka: 4 ciclos,
- Kaida Tema: 4 ciclos,
- Jhup Tal Theka: 2 ciclos,
- Variaciones: 2 ciclos cada una, seguido por 2 ciclos de Jhup Tal theka luego de cada variación.
- Tihai

Jhup Tal – 10 Matras

	+			–		o			–	
	Dhi	na	dhi	dhi	na	tin	na	dhi	dhi	na
	1	2	3	4	5	6	7	8	9	10

Metronome: ♩ = 100

Kaida 6: Theme | *Tema*

	+			–		o			–	
	Dhage	tite	kate	dhage	tina	take	tite	kate	dhage	dhinna
	1	2	3	4	5	6	7	8	9	10

Variations | *Variaciones*

1

+
Dhage tite kate | dhage tite | kate tite kate | dhage tina |

o
take tite kate | dhage tite | kate tite kate | dhage dhinna | }

2

+
Dhage tite dhage | tite dhage | tite tite kate | dhage tina |

o
take tite take | tite dhage | tite tite kate | dhage dhinna | }

3
 +

Dhage tite tite | dhage tite | dhage tite tite | dhage tite |

dhage tite tite | dhage tite | dhage tite kate | dhage dhinna | }

o

take tite tite | take tite | take tite tite | take tite |

dhage tite tite | dhage tite | dhage tite kate | dhage dhinna | }

4
 +

Dhage tite kate | dha dha - tiri | kitetake tirikita dha | dhage tina |

o

take tite kate | ta ta - tiri | kitetake tirikita dha | dhage dhinna | }

5
 +

Dhage tite kate | dhadr drdha | drdr dhadha dhadr | drdha kat - |

o

take tite kata | tatr trta | trtr dhadha dhadr | drdha kat - | }

Tihai

 +

Dhage tite kata | dhadr drdha | dha - dhina dhage | tite kata |

dhadr drdha dha - | dhina dhage | tite kata dhadr | drdha dha - | Dhi ^(+)

Note: The Bol **Dr** *is explained in the 'More Bols for Advance Practice' section on page 88 in this method.*

Nota: El Bol **Dr** *se expone en la sección 'Mas Bols para Practica Avanzada' en la página 88 de este método.*

TRACK
13
DISK
02

Char Tal Ki Sawari
11 Matras, 11 Vibhags

Ricardo Hambra

EXAMPLE 60 – KAIDA 7

- Char Tal Ki Sawari Theka: 4 times,
- Kaida Theme: 4 times,
- Char Tal Ki Sawari Theka: 1 time,
- Variations: 2 times each proceeded by Char Tal Ki Sawari Theka 1 time after each variation.
- Tihai

EJEMPLO 60 – KAIDA 7

- Char Tal Ki Sawari Theka: 4 ciclos,
- Kaida Tema: 4 ciclos,
- Char Tal Ki Sawari Theka: 1 ciclo,
- Variaciones: 2 ciclos cada una, seguido por 1 ciclo de Char Tal Ki Sawari theka luego de cada variación.
- Tihai

Char Tal Ki Sawari – 11 Matras

+			–		–		o		–	–
Dhi - kri	dhita	dhidhi	natrikri	dhita	dhidhi	na - dhage	nadhagena	dhi - ta	- dhi	- ta
1	2	3	4	5	6	7	8	9	10	11

Metronome: ♩ = 100

Kaida 7: Theme | *Tema*

+		–			–		o	–		–
Deredere	kitetake	dha - dha	deredere	kitetake	tu - na	teretere	kitetake	ta - ta	deredere	kitetake
1	2	3	4	5	6	7	8	9	10	11

Variations | *Variaciones*

1

   +   3

(Deredere | kitetake | dha - dha) | deredere | kitetake |

   o   2

(teretere | kitetake | ta - ta) | deredere | kitetake | dha - dha | deredere | kitetake | }

2

   +   3

(Deredere | kitetake) | - - | dha - dha | deredere | kitetake | tu - na |

   o   2

(teretere | kitetake) | deredere | kitetake | - - | dha - dha | deredere | kitetake | dhina | }

3
$^+$ 2
(Deredere | kitetake) | dha - dha | tun - dere | derekite | takedere | derekite | takedha - | dha - tun |

o 2
(teretere | kitetake) | ta - ta | tun - dere | derekite | takedere | derekite | takedha - | dha - dhin | }

4
$^+$
Gidenage | dha - dha | deredere | kitetake | (titetite | dhagena) | kitetake | deredere | kitedha- |
                                                                  2

o 2
kitetake | ta - ta | teretere | kitetake | (titetite | dhagena) | kitetake | deredere | kitedha- | }

Tihai

$^+$ 3x   (+)
[Deredere | kitetake | dha - dha | deredere | kitetake | tu - na | kitetake] | dhanana | Dhi

Note: The Bols **Tri**, **Kri**, **Dere** *and* **Tere** *are explained in the 'More Bols for Advance Practice' section on pages 88 to 91 in this method.*

Nota: Los Bols **Tri**, **Kri**, **Dere** *y* **Tere** *se exponen en detalle en la sección 'Mas Bols para Practica Avanzada' en páginas 88 a 91 de este método*

Ek Tal
12 Matras, 4 Vibhags

Ricardo Hambra

EXAMPLE 61 – KAIDA 8

- Ek Tal Theka: 4 times,
- Kaida Theme: 4 times,
- Ek Tal Theka: 1 time,
- Variations: 2 times each proceeded by Ek Tal Theka 1 time after each variation.
- Tihai

EJEMPLO 61 – KAIDA 8

- Ek Tal Theka: 4 ciclos,
- Kaida Tema: 4 ciclos,
- Ek Tal Theka: 1 ciclo,
- Variaciones: 2 ciclos cada una, seguido por 1 ciclo de Ek Tal Theka luego de cada variación.
- Tihai

Ek Tal – 12 Matras

```
 +                      o              –              –
| Dhi  dhi  dhage  tirikita | tu  na  ka  ta | dhage  tirikita | dhi  na |
  1    2     3       4        5   6   7   8     9      10        11   12
```

Metronome: ♩ = 110

Kaida 8: Theme | *Tema*

```
 +                                  o                                 –                  –
| Dhina  dhina  kitetake  dhina | dhadha  tirikita  tina  tuna | kitetake  dhina | dhadha  tirikita |
   1      2       3        4       5        6        7     8      9        10       11      12
```

Variations | *Variaciones*

```
     +                         3
1  ( Dhina  dhina  kitetake ) dhina | dhadha  tirikita |

     o                  2
   ( tina  tuna  kitetake ) dhina  dhina | kitetake  dhina | dhadha  tirikita | }
```

```
     +
2  Dhina  dhina  kitetake  dhina | dha -  á -  kitetake  tirikita | dha -  dhina | dhadha  tirikita |

     o
   tina  tuna  kitetake  tina | ta -  á -  kitetake  tirikita | dha -  dhina | dhadha  tirikita | }
```

+

3 Dhina dhina kitetake dhina | dhatiri kitetake tirikita dhina | dhatu naka | tadha tirikita |

o

tina tuna kitetake tina | tatiri kitetake tirikita dhina | dhatu naka | tadha tirikita | }

+

4 Dhidhi nana dhidhi nana | dhatiri kitetake tirikite dha - dha - | dhatiri kitadha | dha - tirikita |

o

titi nana tintin nana | tatiri kitetake tirikite ta - ta - | dhatiri kitadha | dha - tirikita | }

Tihai

+   3x (+)

[Dhina dhina kitetake dhina dhadr drdha drdr dhana] Dhi

Deepchandi Tal
14 Matras, 4 Vibhags

Ricardo Hambra

EXAMPLE 62 – KAIDA 9

• Deepchandi Tal Theka: 4 times,
• Kaida Theme: 4 times,
• Deepchandi Tal Theka: 2 times,
• Variations: 2 times each proceeded by Deepchandi Tal Theka 2 times after each variation.
• Tihai

EJEMPLO 62 – KAIDA 9

• Deepchandi Tal Theka: 4 ciclos,
• Kaida Tema: 4 ciclos,
• Deepchandi Tal Theka: 2 ciclos,
• Variaciones: 2 ciclos cada una, seguido por 2 ciclos de Deepchandi Tal Theka luego de cada variación.
• Tihai

Deepchandi Tal – 14 Matras

```
     +              –              o              –
| Dha dhi - | dha ge ti - | ta tin - | dha ge dhi - |
   1   2   3    4   5 6 7   8   9  10   11  12 13 14
```

Metronome: ♩ = 140

Kaida 9: Theme | *Tema*

```
     +                    –                         o                    –
| Dhage na - tina | - dha gena dhage tina | take na - tina | - dha gena dhage dhinna |
    1    2   3      4    5    6     7       8    9   10    11   12    13    14
```

Variations | *Variaciones*

1

```
  +
Dhage na - tina | - dha gena - ti na - | dhage na - tina | - dha gena dhage tina |

  o
take na - tina | - ta kena - ti na - | dhage na - tina | - dha gena dhage dhinna | }
```

2

```
  +
Dhage na - tina | - tiri kitetake tirikita dha - | dhage na - tina | - dha gena dhage tina |

  o
take na - tina | - tiri kitetake tirikita dha - | dhage na - tina | - dha gena dhage dhinna | }
```

+

3   Dhage dhage na - | dhage dhage na - dhina | tirikita dhina tirikita | - dha gena dhage tina |

o

take take na - | dhage dhage na - dhina | tirikita dhina tirikita | - dha gena dhage dhinna | }

+

4   Dhage na - dha - | tirikita taketiri kitadha - - dha | tirikita taketiri kitadha - | - dha gena dhage tina |

o

take na - ta - | tirikita taketiri kitadha - - dha | tirikita taketiri kitadha - | - dha gena dhage dhinna | }

Tihai

+   3x   (+)

[Dhage na - tina tirikita taketa - tirikita taketa - tirikita dha -] dhage | Dha

TRACK
16
DISK
02

Latin Tal
8 Matras, 2 Vibhags

Ricardo Hambra

EXAMPLE 63 – KAIDA 10

- Latin Tal Theka: 4 times,
- Kaida Theme: 4 times,
- Latin Tal Theka: 2 times,
- Variations: 2 times each proceeded by Latin Tal Theka 2 times after each variation.
- Tihai

EJEMPLO 63 – KAIDA 10

- Latin Tal Theka: 4 ciclos,
- Kaida Tema: 4 ciclos,
- Latin Tal Theka: 2 ciclos,
- Variaciones: 2 ciclos cada una, seguido por 2 ciclos de Latin Tal Theka luego de cada variación.
- Tihai

Latin Tal – 8 Matras

+		–		o		–	
Dha -	nage	tita	ketin	- ta	kena	nage	dhina
1	2	3	4	5	6	7	8

Metronome: ♩ = 130

Kaida 10: Theme | *Tema*

+				–				o				–			
Dha -	nage	tita	ketin	- ta	kena	nage	dhina	ta -	nake	tita	keti	- dha	gena	nage	dhinna
1	2	3	4	5	6	7	8	1	2	3	4	5	6	7	8

Variations | *Variaciones*

1

+			3				
(Dha -	nage	tita	ketin)	- ta	kena	nage	dhina

o			2								
(ta -	nake	tita	keti)	dha -	nage	tita	ketin	- dha	gena	nage	dhinna	}

2

+															
Dha -	nage	tita	ketin	dhati	dha -	dhati	dha -	- tiri	ketatake	tiriketa	dha -	- ta	kena	nage	dhina

o															
ta -	nake	tita	keti	tati	ta -	tati	ta -	- tiri	ketatake	tiriketa	dha -	- dha	gena	nage	dhinna	}

3

$\overset{+}{\underline{\text{Dha}}} \text{-} \underline{\text{nage}} \underline{\text{tita}} \underline{\text{ketin}} | (\underline{\text{-take}} \underline{\text{taketita}} \overset{2}{\underline{\text{ketagege}}} \underline{\text{taketina}} \text{-}) | \underline{\text{-ta}} \underline{\text{kena}} \underline{\text{nage}} \underline{\text{dhina}} |$

$\overset{o}{\underline{\text{ta}} \text{-}} \underline{\text{nake}} \underline{\text{tita}} \underline{\text{keti}} | (\underline{\text{-take}} \underline{\text{taketita}} \overset{2}{\underline{\text{ketakeke}}} \underline{\text{taketina}} \text{-}) | \underline{\text{-dha}} \underline{\text{gena}} \underline{\text{nage}} \underline{\text{dhinna}} | \}$

($\underline{\text{gege}}$)

4

$\overset{+}{\underline{\text{Dha}}} \text{-} \underline{\text{nage}} \underline{\text{tita}} \underline{\text{ketin}} | (\underline{\text{dhadr}} \underline{\text{drdha}} \overset{2}{\underline{\text{drdr}}} \underline{\text{dhadha}}) | \underline{\text{-ta}} \underline{\text{kena}} \underline{\text{nage}} \underline{\text{dhina}} |$

$\overset{o}{\underline{\text{ta}} \text{-}} \underline{\text{nake}} \underline{\text{tita}} \underline{\text{keti}} | \underline{\text{tatr}} \underline{\text{trta}} \underline{\text{trtr}} \underline{\text{tata}} | \underline{\text{dhadr}} \underline{\text{drdha}} \underline{\text{drdr}} \underline{\text{dhadha}} | \underline{\text{-dha}} \underline{\text{gena}} \underline{\text{nage}} \underline{\text{dhinna}} | \}$

Tihai*

A

$\overset{+}{\underline{\text{Dha}}} \text{-} \underline{\text{nage}} \underline{\text{tita}} \underline{\text{ketin}} (\underline{\text{-ta}} \underline{\text{kena}} \overset{3 \ (+)}{\underline{\text{nage}}} \underline{\text{dhina}}) \underline{\text{Dha}}$

B

$\overset{+}{[} \underline{\text{Dha}} \text{-} \underline{\text{nage}} \underline{\text{tita}} \underline{\text{ketin}} \underline{\text{dhadr}} \underline{\text{drdha}} \overset{3x \ (+)}{\underline{\text{drdr}}} \underline{\text{dhadha}}] \underline{\text{Dha}}$

* Choose either of these two alternatives to finish the Kaida

* Se puede utilizar cualquiera de estas dos alternativas para terminar el Kaida

TRACK **17** DISK **O2**

Bulería Tal
12 Matras, 5 Vibhags

Ricardo Hambra

EXAMPLE 64 – KAIDA 11

• Bulería Tal Theka: 4 times,
• Kaida Theme: 4 times,
• Bulería Tal Theka: 2 times,
• Variations: 2 times each, but this time, play 1 Theka in between; then proceed with Bulería Tal theka 2 times after each variation.
• Tihai

EJEMPLO 64 – KAIDA 11

• Bulería Tal Theka: 4 ciclos,
• Kaida Tema: 4 ciclos,
• Bulería Tal Theka: 2 ciclos,
• Variaciones: 2 ciclos cada una, pero esta vez con un Theka entre ellos, seguidos por 2 ciclos de Bulería Tal Theka luego de cada variación.
• Tihai

Bulería Tal – 12 Matras

```
(+)
 o        –      –     –     –
│ Ti  te  dha │ ti  te  ti │ dha  dha │ ti  dha │ ti  dha │
  1   2   3     4   5   6    7    8     9   10    1    2
                                              (11) (12)
```

Metronome: ♩ = 200

Kaida 11: Variations | *Variaciones*

```
     o
1  Tiri  kita  dha │ -  -  tiri │ kita  dha │ -  - │ tiri  kita │ } Ti
```

```
     o
2  Dr  dr  dha │ -  -  dr │ dr  dha │ -  - │ dr  dr │ } Ti
```

```
     o                  3   o
3  [ Tite  kata  gadi  gena ]  } Ti
```

```
     o                      2   o
4  [ Dha -  tiri  keta  take  tiri  keta ]  } Ti
```

5
　o　　　　　　　　　　　2　　o
Dhi － na | dhi － na | (take tiri kita) | } Ti

6
　o　　　　　　　　　　　　2　2x
[Dhi － na | dhi － na | (take tiri kita) |] dhi － na | dhi － na | (dha dr dr) | } Ti
　　　　　　　　　　　　　　　　　　　　　　　　　　　　　　　　　2　　o

7
　o　　　3　　　2　o
(Dha tite) (dha dr dr) } Ti

8
　o　　　3　o
[Dha dha dr dr] } Ti

Tihai*

A
　o　　　　　　　　　　3x o
[dr dr dha | － － dr | dr dha | － － | dr dr] Ti

B
　o　　　　　　　　　　　　3x o
[tiri kita dha | － － tiri | kita dha | － － | tiri kita] Ti

* Choose either of these two alternatives to finish the Kaida

* Se puede utilizar cualquiera de estas dos alternativas para terminar el Kaida

Tango Tal
8 Matras, 2 Vibhags

Ricardo Hambra

EXAMPLE 65 – KAIDA 12

- Tango Tal Theka: 4 times,
- Kaida Theme: 4 times,
- Tango Tal Theka: 2 times,
- Variations: 2 times each proceeded by Tango Tal Theka 2 times after each variation.
- Tihai

EJEMPLO 65 – KAIDA 12

- Tango Tal Theka: 4 ciclos,
- Kaida Tema: 4 ciclos,
- Tango Tal Theka: 2 ciclos,
- Variaciones: 2 ciclos cada una, seguido por 2 ciclos de Tango Tal Theka luego de cada variación.
- Tihai

Tango Tal – 8 Matras

```
     +        o        –                 –
 | Dha  ti  te  tirikita | dhina  dhidhi  na  - - |
    1   2   3    4          5      6      7   8
```

Metronome: ♩ = 125

Kaida 12: Theme | *Tema*

```
  +                        –              –        o                  –              –
| Dhati  tedha  tite  dhati | dhati  tedha  tite  tirikita | tati  teta  tite  tati | dhati  tedha  tite  tirikita |
    1      2      3     4       5      6      7      8         1     2     3     4      5      6      7      8
```

Variations | *Variaciones*

```
  +                        3
1 ( Dhati  tedha  tite  dhati ) | dhati  tedha  tite  tirikita |

  o                    2
  ( tati  teta  tite  tati ) | dhati  tedha  tite  dhati | dhati  tedha  tite  tirikita | }
```

```
  +
2 Dhati  tedha  tite  tirikita | tidha  tite  dha  tite | dhati  tedha  tite  tirikita | tidha  tite  dha  tite |

  o
  tati  teta  tite  tirikita | tina  tite  na  tite | dhati  tedha  tite  tirikita | tidha  tite  dha  tite | }
```

3
+
<u>Gege</u> <u>nana</u> <u>gege</u> <u>nana</u> | <u>tite</u> dha <u>tite</u> <u>tirikita</u> | <u>dhati</u> <u>tedha</u> <u>tite</u> <u>tirikita</u> | <u>dhati</u> <u>tedha</u> <u>tite</u> <u>dhina</u> |

o
<u>keke</u> <u>nana</u> <u>keke</u> <u>nana</u> | <u>tite</u> <u>ta</u> <u>tite</u> <u>tirikita</u> | <u>dhati</u> <u>tedha</u> <u>tite</u> <u>tirikita</u> | <u>dhati</u> <u>tedha</u> <u>tite</u> <u>dhinna</u> | }

4
+
<u>Dhati</u> <u>drdr</u> <u>dhati</u> <u>drdr</u> | <u>- dha</u> <u>tite</u> <u>dha</u> <u>tite</u> | <u>dhati</u> <u>drdr</u> <u>dhati</u> <u>drdr</u> | <u>- dha</u> <u>tite</u> <u>dha</u> <u>tite</u> |

o
<u>tati</u> <u>trtr</u> <u>tati</u> <u>trtr</u> | <u>- ta</u> <u>tite</u> <u>ta</u> <u>tite</u> | <u>dhati</u> <u>drdr</u> <u>dhati</u> <u>drdr</u> | <u>- dha</u> <u>tite</u> <u>dha</u> <u>tite</u> | }

5
+
<u>Dhadr</u> <u>drdha</u> <u>drdr</u> <u>dhadr</u> | <u>dhati</u> <u>tedha</u> <u>tite</u> <u>kat</u> | <u>dhadr</u> <u>drdha</u> <u>drdr</u> <u>dhadr</u> | <u>dhati</u> <u>tedha</u> <u>tite</u> <u>kat</u> |

o
<u>tatr</u> <u>trta</u> <u>trtr</u> <u>tatr</u> | <u>tati</u> <u>teta</u> <u>tite</u> <u>ta</u> | <u>dhadr</u> <u>drdha</u> <u>drdr</u> <u>dhadr</u> | <u>dhati</u> <u>tedha</u> <u>tite</u> <u>dhin</u> | }

6
+
<u>Dhati</u> <u>- gena</u> <u>nage</u> <u>tite</u> | <u>dhati</u> <u>- gena</u> <u>nage</u> <u>tite</u> | <u>dhati</u> <u>tedha</u> <u>tite</u> <u>tirikita</u> | <u>dhati</u> <u>tedha</u> <u>tite</u> <u>dhina</u> |

o
<u>tati</u> <u>- kena</u> <u>nake</u> <u>tite</u> | <u>tati</u> <u>- kena</u> <u>nake</u> <u>tite</u> | <u>dhati</u> <u>tedha</u> <u>tite</u> <u>tirikita</u> | <u>dhati</u> <u>tedha</u> <u>tite</u> <u>dhinna</u> | }

7
+   3
(<u>Dhadr</u> <u>drdha</u> <u>drdr</u> <u>dhadr</u>) | <u>dhati</u> <u>tedha</u> <u>tite</u> <u>dhina</u> |

o   2
(<u>tatr</u> <u>trta</u> <u>trtr</u> <u>tatr</u>) | <u>dhadr</u> <u>drdha</u> <u>drdr</u> <u>dhadr</u> | <u>dhati</u> <u>tedha</u> <u>tite</u> <u>dhinna</u> | }

8
+   4   2   2
(<u>Dhadr</u> <u>drdha</u> <u>drdr</u> <u>dhadr</u>) | (<u>tatr</u> <u>trta</u> <u>trtr</u> <u>tatr</u>) | (<u>dhadr</u> <u>drdha</u> <u>drdr</u> <u>dhadr</u>) | }

Tihai

+   (+) 3x
[<u>Dhadr</u> <u>drdha</u> <u>drdr</u> <u>dhadha</u> | <u>drdr</u> <u>dhadr</u> <u>drdha</u> <u>dhadr</u> | <u>drdha</u> <u>drdr</u> <u>Dha</u>]

Samba Tal
8 Matras, 2 Vibhags

Ricardo Hambra

EXAMPLE 66 – KAIDA 13

- Samba Tal Theka: 4 times,
- Kaida Theme: 4 times,
- Samba Tal Theka: 8 times,
- Variations: 2 times each proceeded by Samba Tal Theka 4 times after each variation.
- Tihai

EJEMPLO 66 – KAIDA 13

- Samba Tal Theka: 4 ciclos,
- Kaida Tema: 4 ciclos,
- Samba Tal Theka: 8 ciclos,
- Variaciones: 2 ciclos cada una, seguido por 4 ciclos de Samba Tal Theka luego de cada variación.
- Tihai

Samba Tal – 8 Matras

```
        o         –               –
| Kat  - ta  ge  ta | ka  ta  dita - - |
   1   2   3   4   5   6   7    8
```

Metronome: ♩ = 90

Kaida 13: Theme | *Tema*

```
   o        –                –           o        –               –
| Keti nana ge ge | keti nana gege nana | keti nana ke ke | keti nana gege nana |
   1    2    3  4    5    6    7    8      1    2    3  4    5    6    7    8
```

Variations | *Variaciones*

```
   o
1  Keti nana ge ge | Keti nana gege nana | keti nana ke ke | keti nana gege nana |

   o
   keti nana ke ke | keti nana keke nana | keti nana ge ge | keti nana gege nana | }
```

```
   o
2  Kat tikat - ti kat | ta na - ta kite | tite tite na - tun | tun tirikita ta ke | }
```

o
3 Dha - - - | - - dhita - na | dha - - - | - - - - - |

kat - tin - tin | - na dhita - na | dha - - - | - - - - - | }

o
4 Kat - ta ge ge | ka ta dhige - ge | kat - ta ge ge | ka ta dhige - ge |

o
kat - ta ke ke | ka ta tike - ke | kat - ta ge ge | ka ta dhige - ge | }

o
5 Kati ta geti ta | kati ta gege ta | kati ta geti ta | kati ta gege ta |

o
kati ta keti ta | kati ta keke ta | kati ta geti ta | kati ta gege ta | }

o
6 Ka kat dha - ta | keta - ta geta tite | ka kat dha - ta | keta - ta geta tite |

o
ka kat ta - ta | keta - ta keta tite | ka kat dha - ta | keta - ta geta tite | }

o
7 Dhadr drdr dhadr drdr | ka ta dhita - | dhadr drdr dhadr drdr | ka ta dhita - |

o
tatr trtr tatr trtr | ka ta tita - | dhadr drdr dhadr drdr | ka ta dhita - | }

o   3   3
8 (Dhadr drdr dhadr drdr) | ka ta dhita - | (dhadr drdr dhadr drdr) | ka ta dhita - |

o   3   3
(tatr trtr tatr trtr) | ka ta tita - | (dhadr drdr dhadr drdr) | ka ta dhita - | }

Tihai

o   3x   +(o)
[Kat tikat - ti kat | ta na - ta kite | tite tite na -] tun tun tirikita ta na | Kat

MORE BOLS FOR ADVANCED PRACTICE

MÁS BOLS PARA PRÁCTICA AVANZADA

DR: The Bol **DR** is a combination of **TITE** and **KE** played in a very fast sequence. It sounds like the **TIRIKI** of Bol **TIRIKITA**, which has been explained earlier in the '*Combined Bols*' section of this method.

DR: El Bol **DR** es una combinación del **TITE** y el **KE**, tocado de forma muy rápida. Se puede relacionar con el **TIRIKI** del Bol **TIRIKITA**, analizado anteriormente en la sección '*Bols Combinados*' de este método.

EXAMPLE 67: DR

EJEMPLO 67: DR

TI  **TE**  **KE**

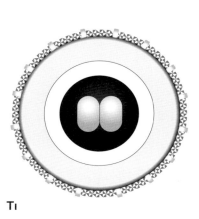 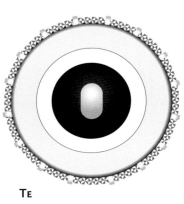 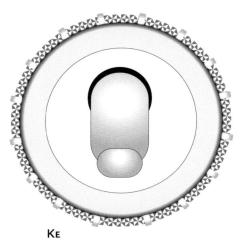

TI   TE   KE

DERE & TERE

DERE & TERE

DERE: This stroke is also performed as a combined Bol. First we have a Bol **DE**, which is a combination of **GE + TE** played with both hands simultaneously. In this case, the Bol **TE** is played with the outer part of the hand (little finger side), as shown in the graphic and picture.

Then comes the Bol **RE**, which is always played following the **DE** in the Dayan drum alone; this Bol is played with the inner part of the hand (thumb side), as shown below. The combination of both strokes produces the Bol called **DERE**.

DERE: Este golpe también hace parte de los Bols combinados. Primero está el Bol **DE**, que es una combinación de **GE + TE** tocado de forma simultánea con ambas manos. En éste caso el **TE** se toca golpeando con la zona exterior de la mano, del lado del dedo meñique, como lo muestran las imágenes y gráficos.

Luego está el Bol **RE**, el cual se toca siempre siguiendo al **DE**, pero solo en el Dayan, golpeando con la parte interior de la mano, utilizando la zona del dedo pulgar. La combinación de ambos golpes produce el Bol **DERE**.

EXAMPLE 68: DERE

EJEMPLO 67: DERE

TRACK
21
DISK
02

GE

TE

RE

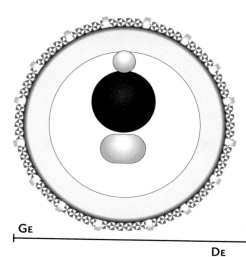

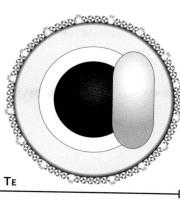

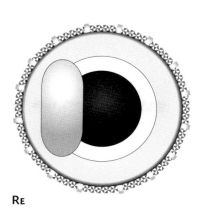

GE

TE

DE

RE

TERE: In the case of **TERE**, it is performed with the Dayan drum alone, without the use of **GE**, as shown below:

TERE: En el caso del Bol **TERE**, éste se toca en el tambor Dayan solamente, sin usar el **GE** como en el caso del **DERE**:

EXAMPLE 68: TERE

EJEMPLO 68: TERE

TRACK
21
DISK
02

TE

RE

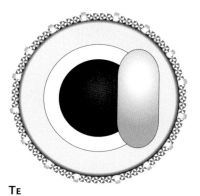

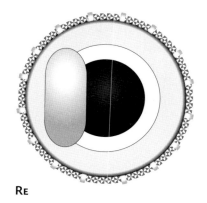

TE

RE

TRIK: Hitting the Dayan head with the ring, middle and index fingers, in a very short and quick sequence, produces this stroke. See the pictures below:

EXAMPLE 69: TRIK

TRIK: Este Bol se produce golpeando el Dayan con los dedos anular, medio e índice, en una muy rápida secuencia, tal como lo muestran las imágenes y el gráfico.

EJEMPLO 69: TRIK

1. RING | *ANULAR* **2. MIDDLE | *MEDIO*** **3. INDEX | *ÍNDICE***

TRIK

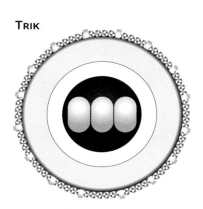

TRIKRI

TRI: Hitting the Dayan head with the ring, middle and index fingers, in a very short and quick sequence, followed by the stroke **KE** on the Bayan, produces the Bol **TRI**. See the pictures below:

EXAMPLE 70: TRI

TRIKRI

TRI: Este bol se produce golpeando el Dayan con los dedos anular, medio e índice, en una muy rápida secuencia, seguido del Bol **KE**, tal como lo muestran las imágenes y gráfico.

EJEMPLO 70: TRI

1. RING | *ANULAR* **2. MIDDLE | *MEDIO*** **3. INDEX | *ÍNDICE*** **4. KE**

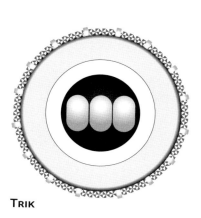

TRIK

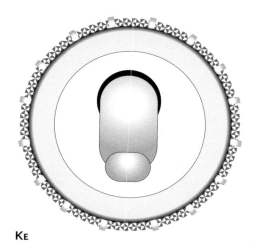

KE

KRI: Hitting the stroke **KE** on the Bayan head followed by the Dayan Bol **TRIK**, produces **KRI**. See the pictures below:

KRI: Este Bol se produce golpeando el Bol **KE**, seguido del Bol **TRIK**, o sea, en el orden inverso del **TRI** explicado anteriormente. Ver imágenes y gráfico.

EXAMPLE 70: KRI

EJEMPLO 70: KRI

TRACK
23
DISK
02

1. KE

2. RING | *ANULAR*

3. MIDDLE | *MEDIO*

4. INDEX | *ÍNDICE*

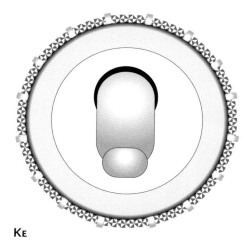

KE

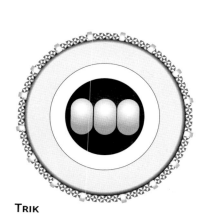

TRIK

GRAPHIC ILLUSTRATIONS OF THE TABLA DRUMS, ALONG WITH THE NAMES OF ITS DIFFERENT COMPONENTS

ILUSTRACIONES GRÁFICAS DEL TABLA, JUNTO A LOS NOMBRES DE SUS DISTINTOS COMPONENTES

DAYAN DRUM PARTS

PARTES DEL DAYAN

Gajra
Drumhead skin
Piel o parche

Chot
Leather cord
Cuerda de cuero

Gattha
Wooden cylinders
Cilindros de madera

Gurri
Leather ring
Anillo de cuero, base

Adhara
Cushion
Cojín

BAYAN DRUM PARTS

PARTES DEL BAYAN

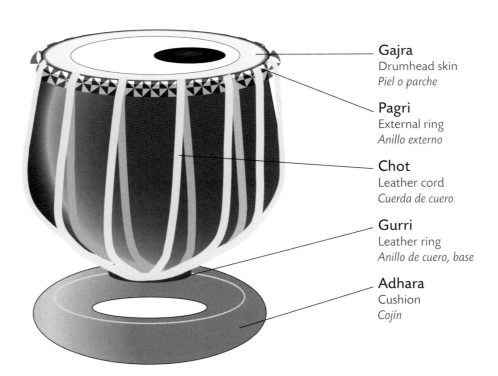

Gajra
Drumhead skin
Piel o parche

Pagri
External ring
Anillo externo

Chot
Leather cord
Cuerda de cuero

Gurri
Leather ring
Anillo de cuero, base

Adhara
Cushion
Cojín

GLOSSARY

Adharas: Circular cushions on which the Dayan and Bayan drums rest.

Bayan: Low pitch drum of the Tabla set, also called *Duggi*, *Dugga*, among other names.

Bol: Stroke, group of strokes or an entire composition based on rhythmic phrases.

Carnatic: Name referred to the South Indian music theory system.

Chakradar: The Sanskrit word *Chakra* means 'Wheel' or 'Spin', therefore Chakradar could be translated as 'Spinning Tihai'. It often indicates the conclusion of an entire performance or composition.

Chot: Leather cord that is used to hold the drumhead to the body of the Tabla drum.

Dayan: High pitch drum of the Tabla set, also called *Tabla*.

Gajra or **Drumhead**: Skin, Head, Top. A membrane which covers the drum and produces a sound by its percussion.

Gharana: Family or School. In India, it is a tradition that sons continue their ancestor's profession. With this intention the Gharanas were created. It has also included disciples and fans. Gharanas are named depending on the founder's birthplace.

Gurri: Bottom leather ring that is used to hold the leather cord of each drum.

Gattha: Wooden cylinders that are used to tune the Dayan.

Industani: Name used to call the North Indian music theory system, which could also be written as *Hindustani*. I have chosen to refer at it as *Industani*, because in my research I have learned that this system has been developed in what was called at ancient times the Indus Valley area, while the term Hindustani makes a reference to the Hindu religion.

Kaida: This word means 'Law' or 'Code'. Previously written composition based on one Tala or rhythmic cycle.

Khali: Secondary accent of a Tala or rhythmic cycle.

Kinar: External circle of the Dayan and Bayan drumhead.

Lay: Means 'Speed' or 'Tempo' for each music performance or composition. There are 3 standard Lay Categories: *Vilambit* or Slow tempo, *Madhya* or Medium tempo and *Drut* or Fast tempo.

Matra: Time measure unit of a Tala or rhythmic cycle.

Mridangam: Percussion instrument mostly used in South India, also called *Mirdangam*, *Mridanga* or *Mrindangam*.

Pagri: External ring of the Dayan and Bayan drumhead.

Pakhawaj: Percussion instrument that is said to be the ancestor of the Tabla.

Raga: Melodic matrix with particular characteristics, used in almost every traditional Indian music composition.

Sam: Main or principal accent of a Tala.

Sarod: Stringed instrument that's used mostly in North India and Pakistan.

Shadaja or **Sa**: Basic note of the Indian traditional music notation system.

Shyahi: Central black circle of the Dayan and Bayan drumheads.

Sitar: Stringed instrument mostly used in the Industani traditional music.

Sur: Medium circle of the Dayan and Bayan drumheads.

GLOSARIO

Adharas: Cojines circulares en los que se apoyan el Dayan y el Bayan.

Bayan: Tambor grave del Tabla, también llamado *Duggi*, *Dugga*, entre otros nombres.

Bol: Golpe, grupo de golpes, o composición basada en frases rítmicas.

Carnatic: Karnataka es el nombre del sistema teórico de música, característico del Sur de la India.

Chakradar: *Chakra* significa en sánscrito 'rueda' o 'giro', chakradar por lo tanto se traduciría 'giro sobre giro', este es el sentido del Chakradar Tihai, y es casi siempre el que marca el final completo de una obra.

Chot: Cuerda o tiento de cuero utilizada para afianzar los parches al cuerpo del Tabla.

Dayan: Tambor agudo del Tabla, también llamado *Tabla*.

Gajra o **Parche**: Piel, cabeza. Membrana que recubre el tambor y produce el sonido mediante su percusión.

Gharana: Familia o escuela. En India es costumbre que los hijos hereden la profesión de sus padres. Con esta intención se han ido creando estos Gharanas, incluyendo discípulos y adeptos. Los Gharanas son nombrados según el lugar donde reside su fundador, el más antiguo miembro de la familia.

Gurri: Anillo de cuero ubicado en la parte inferior del tambor; se utiliza para entrelazar el tiento de cuero.

Gattha: Cilindros de madera utilizados para afinar el Dayan.

Indostánico: Nombre que se utiliza para el sistema teórico de música, característico del Norte de la India, el cual también puede ser escrito *Hindostánico*. He elegido el termino *Indostánico* porque durante mis estudios pude aprender que este sistema musical fue desarrollado en lo que en tiempos antiguos se llamaba la zona del Valle del Indo, mientras que el termino Hindostánico se refiere a lo relacionado con la religión Hindú.

Kaida: Palabra persa que significa 'ley' o 'código'. Composición escrita previamente basada en un Tal.

Khali: Acento secundario de un Tal.

Kinar: Círculo exterior del parche del Dayan y Bayan.

Lay: Significa 'velocidad' o 'tempo' para cada composición o interpretación. En música India se consideran 3 tipos de velocidad básicas, *Vilambit* o lenta; *Madhya* o normal y *Drut* o rápida.

Matra: Unidad de tiempo en la medición de un Tal o ciclo rítmico.

Mridangam: Instrumento de percusión característico del Sur de India, también llamado *Mirdangam*, *Mridanga* o *Mrindangam*.

Pagri: Anillo externo del parche del Dayan y Bayan.

Pakhawaj: Instrumento de percusión que se dice fue el antecesor del Tabla.

Raga: Matriz melódica con características o giros particulares, utilizada en gran parte de las composiciones en la música tradicional de la India.

Sam: Acento más importante de un Tal.

Sarod: Instrumento de cuerda utilizado en el Norte de India y Pakistán.

Shadaja o **Sa**: Nota básica de la notación melódica en música tradi-

Tal or **Tala** (pl. **Talas**): Rhythmic Cycle. A fixed number of time units that conforms a cyclic pattern.

Tali: Minor accent of a Tal

That: pronounce Tut, name of a melodic scale in the Industani music system.

Tihai: a fixed pattern of three identical phrases that indicates a transition to another movement inside a composition, or a finale of an entire composition.

Vibhag: Bar or measure. A specific subdivision within a Tala or rhythmic cycle.

cional de India.

Shyahi: Círculo central – negro – del Dayan y Bayan.

Sitar: Instrumento de cuerdas utilizado en la música tradicional Indostánica.

Sur: Círculo medio del parche del Dayan y Bayan.

Tal o **Tala** (pl. **Talas**): Ciclo rítmico. Número fijo de unidades de tiempo que forman un patrón cíclico.

Tali: Acento menor de un Tal.

That: Pronunciar Tat; nombre de una escala melódica dentro del sistema musical Indostánico.

Tihai: Un patrón fijo de tres frases idénticas, que indica la transición hacia otro movimiento dentro de una composición, o la conclusión o final de una composición.

Vibhag: Compás. Agrupamiento específico en subdivisiones más pequeñas de un Tal o ciclo rítmico.

RESOURCES

Here are some books and learning methods I have the opportunity to come across, though few in number, but very important for the accomplishment of this method:

- *Learning Tabla with Ustad Alla Rakha*
- *42 Lessons for Tabla*, by Ustad Keramatullah Khan
- *The Major Traditions of North Indian Tabla Drumming,* by Robert Gottlieb
- *Learn to Play Tabla*, by Ram Avtar Vir

FUENTES DE INFORMACIÓN

Estos son algunos títulos de libros y métodos de aprendizaje que he tenido la oportunidad de encontrar. Si bien son pocos en cantidad, han servido mucho para la realización de este método:

- *Learning Tabla with Ustad Alla Rakha*
- *42 Lessons for Tabla*, por Ustad Keramatullah Khan
- *The Major Traditions of North Indian Tabla Drumming,* por Robert Gottlieb
- *Learn to Play Tabla*, por Ram Avtar Vir

RICARDO HAMBRA

I am basically a Music fan. I've listened to lots of beautiful music from everywhere. Having said that, my musical studies and professional experience as a musician, percussionist and singer, have taken me to many parts of the world, bringing me into contact with a rich variety of cultures and musical currents.

I've been studying and doing research about Ethnic and Modern music for more than 15 years, through undergraduate studies, workshops, masterclasses, traveling around the world, and learning from teachers and local artists in their towns.

India, Africa, Middle East, Eastern and Western Europe, North, Central and South America, Australia, Asia. It is an invaluable experience what is possible to learn and also share through music and the different cultures of the world.

Maybe I should describe my musical influences by stages:

I started to play music at 7: Bombo Legüero, an ethnic Argentinean Percussion instrument; then at 13 one of my uncles made me a present of a Drum set, which was a big push for a further career as a percussionist.

Soon after came my first Rock and Blues high school band. After that, Symphonic Rock, Jazz Rock, Jazz Fusion, Funk, Pop and Reggae music came to my attention.

Then I discovered India, which was definitely a decisive influence in both my music career and personal life. It is because of this influence that I am able to achieve the production of this method, and I am very grateful for it.

Nevertheless, I kept my original empathy for world music styles. I have traveled around Argentina, Brazil, Uruguay, Chile, Mexico and USA, learning different styles like: Tango, Samba, Bossa, Latin Salsa, Afro Cuban and Andean music, plus Jazz, Blues, Country, etc. All of this was of great influence.

Later I started to do more research about Eastern Europe and Mediterranean music, and I worked playing Middle-eastern, Greek, Rumanian, Bulgarian, Sefardi, Celtic and especially Spanish Flamenco music, touring with several music and Dance groups for many years during my time in Madrid.

By the time of the conclusion of *Tabla for All*, I spend most of the time in Los Angeles, USA as a performing musician, producer and teacher, and also leading my own music productions company, called **Ethnic Fusion Sound**.

www.ethnicfusionsound.com

Foto © Ricardo Hambra

RICARDO HAMBRA

Básicamente, soy un fan de la Música. He escuchado hermosas piezas de todo el mundo. Dicho esto, mis estudios musicales así como mi experiencia como músico, percusionista y cantante, además de productor y profesor, me han llevado a distintos lugares alrededor del mundo, poniéndome en contacto con una variedad rica de culturas e influencias musicales.

He estado estudiando e investigando sobre músicas del mundo y la relación entre la música étnica y moderna, por mas de 15 años, a través de estudios terciarios, cursos, clases magistrales, viajes por el mundo y aprendiendo tanto de maestros, así como de artistas locales que viven en la cotidianidad de sus culturas.

India, África, Mediterráneo, Europa del Este y el Oeste, América del Norte, Centro y Sur, Australia, Asia. Es invalorable lo que se puede aprender y compartir a través de la música y las diversas culturas del mundo.

Quizás deba describir mis influencias musicales por etapas:

Comencé a los 7 años con el Bombo Legüero, instrumento de percusión étnica de Argentina, luego a los 13 uno de mis tíos me obsequió mi primera Batería, dándome un fuerte impulso hacia una posterior vocación como percusionista.

Luego integre mi primer banda de Rock & Blues en la escuela secundaria. Posteriormente vino el Rock Sinfónico, Jazz Rock, Jazz Fusión, Funk, Pop y el Reggae, estilos que me fueron despertando la curiosidad por los ritmos del mundo.

Mas tarde descubrí la India y su música, lo cual fue una influencia decisiva tanto en lo musical como a nivel personal. Es gracias a ello que he logrado concretar la producción de este método, lo cual agradezco mucho.

He continuado sin embargo con mi empatía original hacia las músicas del mundo, viajando por Argentina Brasil, Chile, Uruguay, México y EEUU, donde he entrado en contacto con diferentes estilos musicales como Tango, Samba, Bossa, Música Latina (salsa), Afro Cubana y Andina, Jazz, Blues, Country, etc. Todo ha sido de gran beneficio.

Más tarde comencé a investigar sobre la música de Europa del Este y el Mediterráneo, lo cual me llevó a trabajar con música del Medio Oriente, Grecia, Bulgaria, Rumania, Sefardí, Celta, y especialmente el Flamenco de España; colaborando durante años con diversos grupos de música y danza en mi paso por Madrid.

Para el momento en que finalizo *Tabla para Todos*, continuo mi trabajo en Los Angeles, Estados Unidos como músico profesional, docente y productor.

Además, coordino mi propia productora musical llamada **Ethnic Fusion Sound**.

www.ethnicfusionsound.com

CD CONTENTS

CD1
Track   Page

MUSICA EN CD

CD1
Track   Página

CD2
Track
Page

CHAPTER III

CD2
Track
Página

CAPÍTULO III

MUSICIANS

Ricardo Hambra: Tabla set, vocal percussion
Aditya Varnam: Tampura tracks

Recording, Mixing and Mastering:
Ricardo Hambra
Recorded at *EFS* Studios, Los Angeles, California, USA.

MÚSICOS

Ricardo Hambra: Set de Tabla, percusión vocal
Aditya Varnam: Pistas de Tampura

Grabación, mezcla y masterización:
Ricardo Hambra
Grabado en los Estudios *EFS*, en la ciudad de Los Ángeles, California, Estados Unidos.